Y0-BCW-166

Ready, Set, Go!™

Algebra & Functions

Workbook

Mel Friedman, M.S.

For **New Jersey HSPA**

Research & Education Association
Visit our website at
www.rea.com

Research & Education Association
61 Ethel Road West
Piscataway, New Jersey 08854
E-mail: info@rea.com

REA's Ready, Set, Go!™
Algebra and Functions Workbook
for the New Jersey High School Proficiency Assessment (HSPA)

Copyright © 2009 by Research & Education Association, Inc.
All rights reserved. No part of this book may be reproduced
in any form without the permission of the publisher.

Printed in the United States of America

ISBN-13: 978-0-7386-0521-0
ISBN-10: 0-7386-0521-2

LIMIT OF LIABILITY/DISCLAIMER OF WARRANTY: Publication of this work is for
the purpose of test preparation and related use and subjects as set forth herein.
While every effort has been made to achieve a work of high quality, neither
Research & Education Association, Inc., nor the authors and other contributors
of this work guarantee the accuracy or completeness of or assume any liability
in connection with the information and opinions contained herein. REA and
the authors and other contributors shall in no event be liable for any personal
injury, property or other damages of any nature whatsoever, whether special,
indirect, consequential or compensatory, directly or indirectly resulting from
the publication, use or reliance upon this work.

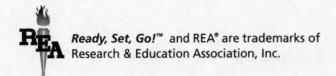

Ready, Set, Go!™ and REA® are trademarks of
Research & Education Association, Inc.

Contents

About Research & Education Association

Founded in 1959, Research & Education Association (REA) is dedicated to publishing the finest and most effective educational materials—including software, study guides, and test preps—for students in elementary school, middle school, high school, college, graduate school, and beyond.

Today, REA's wide-ranging catalog is a leading resource for teachers, students, and professionals.

We invite you to visit us at *www.rea.com* to find out how "REA is making the world smarter."

About the Author

Author Mel Friedman is a former classroom teacher and test-item writer for Educational Testing Service and ACT, Inc.

Acknowledgments

We would like to thank Larry Kling, Vice President, Editorial, for his editorial direction; Pam Weston, Vice President, Publishing, for setting the quality standards for production integrity and managing the publication to completion; Alice Leonard, Senior Editor, for project management and preflight editorial review; Diane Goldschmidt, Senior Editor, for post-production quality assurance; Ruth O'Toole, Production Editor, for proofreading; Rachel DiMatteo, Graphic Artist, for page design; Christine Saul, Senior Graphic Artist, for cover design; and Jeff LoBalbo, Senior Graphic Artist, for post-production file mapping.

We also gratefully acknowledge Heather Brashear for copyediting, and Kathy Caratozzolo of Caragraphics for typesetting.

Our sincere gratitude is extended to longtime math tutor, teacher, and author Bob Miller for his review of all test items.

A special thank you to Mary Berlinghieri and the students of Union Catholic High School in Scotch Plains, New Jersey, for reviewing and field-testing lessons from this book.

Welcome
to the *Ready, Set, Go!*
Algebra & Functions Workbook!

About This Book

This book will help high school math students at all learning levels understand basic algebra. Students will develop the skills, confidence, and knowledge they need to succeed on high school math exams with emphasis on passing high school graduation exams.

More than 20 easy-to-follow lessons break down the material into the basics. In-depth, step-by-step examples and solutions reinforce student learning, while the "Math Flash" feature provides useful tips and strategies, including advice on common mistakes to avoid.

Students can take drills and quizzes to test themselves on the subject matter, then review any areas in which they need improvement or additional reinforcement. The book concludes with a final exam, designed to comprehensively test what students have learned.

The *Ready, Set, Go! Algebra & Functions Workbook* will help students master the basics of mathematics—and help them face their next math test—with confidence!

Icons Explained

Icons make navigating through the book easier. The icons, explained below, highlight tips and strategies, where to review a topic, and the drills found at the end of each lesson.

Look for the **"Math Flash"** feature for helpful tips and strategies, including advice on how to avoid common mistakes.

When you see the **"Let's Review"** icon, you know just where to look for more help with the topic on which you are currently working.

The **"Test Yourself!"** icon, found at the end of every lesson, signals a short drill that reviews the skills you have studied in that lesson.

To the Student

This workbook will help you master the fundamentals of Algebra & Functions. It offers you the support you need to boost your skills and helps you succeed in school and beyond!

It takes the guesswork out of math by explaining what you most need to know in a step-by-step format. When you apply what you learn from this workbook, you can

1. **do better in class;**
2. **raise your grades, and**
3. **score higher on your high school math exams.**

Each compact lesson in this book introduces a math concept and explains the method behind it in plain language. This is followed with lots of examples with fully worked-out solutions that take you through the key points of each problem.

The book gives you two tools to measure what you learn along the way:

✔ **Short drills that follow <u>each</u> lesson**
✔ **Quizzes that test you on <u>multiple</u> lessons**

These tools are designed to comfortably build your test-taking confidence.

Meanwhile, the "Math Flash" feature throughout the book offers helpful tips and strategies—including advice on how to avoid common mistakes.

When you complete the lessons, take the final exam at the end of the workbook to see how far you've come. If you still need to strengthen your grasp on any concept, you can always go back to the related lesson and review at your own pace.

To the Parent

For many students, math can be a challenge—but with the right tools and support, your child can master the basics of algebra. As educational publishers, our goal is to help all students develop the crucial math skills they'll need in school and beyond.

This **Ready, Set, Go! Workbook** is intended for students who need to build their basic algebra skills. It was specifically created and designed to assist students who need a boost in understanding and learning the math concepts that are most tested along the path to graduation. Through a series of easy-to-follow lessons, students are introduced to the essential mathematical ideas and methods, and then take short quizzes to test what they are learning.

Each lesson is devoted to a key mathematical building block. The concepts and methods are fully explained, then reinforced with examples and detailed solutions. Your child will be able to test what he or she has learned along the way, and then take a cumulative exam found at the end of the book.

Whether used in school with teachers, for home study, or with a tutor, the ***Ready, Set, Go! Workbook*** is a great support tool. It can help improve your child's math proficiency in a way that's fun and educational!

To the Teacher

As you know, not all students learn the same, or at the same pace. And most students require additional instruction, guidance, and support in order to do well academically.

Using the Curriculum Focal Points of the National Council of Teachers of Mathematics, this workbook was created to help students increase their math abilities and succeed on high school exams with special emphasis on high school proficiency exams. The book's easy-to-follow lessons offer a review of the basic material, supported by examples and detailed solutions that illustrate and reinforce what the students have learned.

To accommodate different pacing for students, we provide drills and quizzes throughout the book to enable students to mark their progress. This approach allows for the mastery of smaller chunks of material and provides a greater opportunity to build mathematical competence and confidence.

When we field-tested this series in the classroom, we made every effort to ensure that the book would accommodate the common need to build basic math skills as effectively and flexibly as possible. Therefore, this book can be used in conjunction with lesson plans, stand alone as a single teaching source, or be used in a group-learning environment. The practice quizzes and drills can be given in the classroom as part of the overall curriculum or used for independent study. A cumulative exam at the end of the workbook helps students (and their instructors) gauge their mastery of the subject matter.

We are confident that this workbook will help your students develop the necessary skills and build the confidence they need to succeed on high school math exams.

Variables and Algebraic Expressions in One Variable

In this lesson, we will explore the meaning of algebraic expressions or an equation that has one unknown. This is represented by a letter. These letters are called variables. You will see that an expression with a variable can be solved when you are given the value of the variable.

Your Goal: When you have completed this lesson, you should be able to determine the value of any algebraic expression involving one variable.

LESSON 1

Variables and Algebraic Expressions in One Variable

Algebraic expressions contain a combination of letters (called variables) and numbers (called constants). These variables and constants are joined together using any or all of the arithmetic operations. These include addition, subtraction, multiplication, division, and exponents. The variables represent unknown quantities. Usually, letters such as x, y, and z are used to represent unknown quantities; however, there is no strict rule as to which letters may be used. In this lesson, we will just use either x, y, or z to represent the unknown quantity. Remember that whenever you see a variable such as x, it means $1 \cdot x$, usually written as $1x$. Caution: This does <u>not</u> mean that the value of x is 1.

1

Example: *Evaluate $x + 10$, given that $x = -3$.*

Solution: When we insert -3 for the x, we get $-3 + 10 = 7$. (When we combine two numbers that have unlike signs, we subtract. We keep the sign of the larger number.)

2

Example: *Evaluate $8 - 2x$, given that $x = 5$.*

Solution: When we substitute 5 for the x, we get $8 - (2)(5) = 8 - 10 = -2$.

3

Example: *Evaluate $-13 - x$, given that $x = 17$.*

Solution: When we substitute 17 for the x, we get $-13 - 17 = -30$. (When we combine two numbers that have the same signs, we add and keep that sign.)

Example: *Evaluate –4x – 9, given that* $x = -\dfrac{3}{8}$.

4

Solution: When we substitute $-\dfrac{3}{8}$ for x, we get

$$(-4)\left(-\dfrac{3}{8}\right) - 9 = \dfrac{12}{8} - 9 = \dfrac{3}{2} - 9 = \dfrac{3}{2} - \dfrac{18}{2} = -\dfrac{15}{2}.$$

Example: *Evaluate* $\dfrac{y}{6} + 9$, *given that y = –42.*

5

Solution: When we substitute –42 for y, we get $\dfrac{-42}{6} + 9 = -7 + 9 = 2$.

Example: *Evaluate* $\dfrac{10}{w} - 11$, *given that w = –0.8.*

6

Solution: By substitution, we get $\dfrac{10}{-0.8} - 11 = -12.5 - 11 = -23.5$.

Example: *Evaluate –z² + 25, given that z = 0.4.*

7

Solution: By substitution, $-(0.4)^2 + 25 = -0.16 + 25 = 24.84$. Hopefully, you remembered that $-(0.4)^2 = -(0.4)(0.4)$, and that the negative sign preceding the parentheses makes $-(0.4)^2$ a negative number.

Example: *Evaluate –4y² +6y –2, given that* $y = -\dfrac{1}{3}$.

8

Solution: By substitution, $(-4)\left(-\dfrac{1}{3}\right)^2 + (6)\left(-\dfrac{1}{3}\right) - 2 = (-4)\left(\dfrac{1}{9}\right) - 2 - 2 =$

$-\dfrac{4}{9} - 4 = -\dfrac{4}{9} - \dfrac{36}{9} = -\dfrac{40}{9}$. (Note that we changed –4 to $-\dfrac{36}{9}$.)

9

Example: *Evaluate $z^2 + 4z - 7$, given that $z = 3$.*

Solution: By substitution, $(3)^2 + (4)(3) - 7 = 9 + 12 - 7 = 14$.

10

Example: *Evaluate $(6w)^2 + 10w - 32$, given that $w = \dfrac{2}{3}$.*

Solution: By substitution, $\left(6 \times \dfrac{2}{3}\right)^2 + (10)\left(\dfrac{2}{3}\right) - 32 = (4)^2 + \dfrac{20}{3} - 32 =$

$16 + \dfrac{20}{3} - 32 = \dfrac{48}{3} + \dfrac{20}{3} - \dfrac{96}{3} = -\dfrac{28}{3}$.

MathFlash!

$$(6w)^2 \neq 6w^2$$

On the left side, we first multiply 6 by w, then square this result; on the right side, we square w first, then multiply this number by 6. Suppose w = 2. $(6 \times 2)^2 = 12^2 = 144$. However, $6(2)^2 = 6 \times 4 = 24$. They are <u>not</u> equal!

Test Yourself!

Evaluate each algebraic expression with the given value of the variable.

1. $x + 7$, given that $x = -1.6$ *Answer:* _____

2. $22 - 5x$, given that $x = 9$ *Answer:* _____

3. $\dfrac{8}{x} + 24$, given that $x = -5$ *Answer:* _____

4. $-21z - 19$, given that $z = -1$ *Answer:* _____

5. $9y + \dfrac{y^2}{2}$, given that $y = 10$ *Answer:* _____

6. $-y^2 + 10y - 1$, given that $y = \dfrac{1}{2}$ *Answer:* _____

7. $\dfrac{z}{-5} + 12$, given that $z = 75$ *Answer:* _____

8. $(3w)^2 - 7w$, given that $w = -3$ *Answer:* _____

9. $\dfrac{2}{w} - 5w + 8$, given that $w = -\dfrac{1}{5}$ *Answer:* _____

10. $4y^2 + 2$, given that $y = 0.9$ *Answer:* _____

Linear Equations in One Variable—Part 1

In this lesson, we will explore the methods to solve a linear equation in one variable. Each of these equations will have a single answer, also called a solution. As in Lesson 1, we will use the letters *x, y,* or *z* to represent the unknown quantity; however, you need to understand that any letter may be used.

Your Goal: When you have completed this lesson, you should be able to determine the solution of a linear equation for which there is exactly one solution. In a later lesson, we will work on linear equations for which there is either no solution or infinitely many solutions.

LESSON 2

Linear Equations in One Variable— Part 1

As we proceed through this lesson, you need to know that an equation represents a balance of two equal quantities. Basically, this means that the left side must be equal to the right side. For a linear equation, the highest exponent of the given variable will be 1. In each equation, the letter x will be used. (Any letter would be allowed.)

1

Example: *What is the value of x in the equation 3x = 33?*

Solution: In this equation, 3 is multiplied by x. To solve for x, divide both sides of the equation by 3. Then $\frac{3x}{3} = \frac{33}{3}$, so $x = 11$.

2

Example: *What is the value of x in the equation x + 11 = 7 ?*

Solution: Since x is added to 11, we subtract 11 on both sides of the equation. Then $x + 11 - 11 = 7 - 11$, so $x = -4$.

3

Example: *What is the value of x in the equation x – 22 = –5?*

Solution: Since x is subtracted by 22, we must add 22 to both sides of the equation. Then $x - 22 + 22 = -5 + 22$, so $x = 17$.

4

Example: *What is the value of x in the equation $\frac{x}{5}$ = 9?*

Solution: In this equation, x is already divided by 5. To find x, we multiply both sides of the equation by 5. Then $\left(\frac{x}{5}\right)(5) = (9)(5)$, so $x = 45$.

5

Example: *What is the value of x in the equation –8x = –2?*

Solution: Since x is multiplied by –8, we must divide both sides of the equation by –8. Careful: Do <u>not</u> write the answer as 4! The correct answer will be $\frac{-2}{-8}$, which reduces to $\frac{1}{4}$. **(Remember that when dividing two negative numbers, the answer is positive.)** Then $\frac{-8x}{-8} = \frac{-2}{-8}$, so $x = \frac{1}{4}$.

6

Example: *What is the value of x in the equation $x + \frac{7}{4} = -\frac{1}{6}$?*

Solution: Similar to Example 5, we must subtract $\frac{7}{4}$ from both sides of the equation. $x + \frac{7}{4} - \frac{7}{4} = -\frac{1}{6} - \frac{7}{4}$. Thus, $x = -\frac{1}{6} - \frac{7}{4} = -\frac{2}{12} - \frac{21}{12} = -\frac{23}{12}$.

7

Example: *What is the value of x in the equation $x - 4 = -\frac{7}{8}$?*

Solution: Similar to Example 6, we must add 4 to both sides of the equation. $x - 4 + 4 = -\frac{7}{8} + 4$. Thus, $x = -\frac{7}{8} + 4 = -\frac{7}{8} + \frac{32}{8} = \frac{25}{8}$. $\left(\text{Note that } 4 = \frac{32}{8}.\right)$

8

Example: *What is the value of x in the equation $\frac{x}{6} = \frac{3}{4}$?*

Solution: One way to handle this problem is to recognize its similarity to Example 4. Since x is already divided by 6, we must multiply both sides of the equation by 6. $(6)\left(\frac{x}{6}\right) = (6)\left(\frac{3}{4}\right)$. Then $x = (6)\left(\frac{3}{4}\right) = \frac{18}{4}$, which can be reduced to $\frac{9}{2}$ or 4.5. Another approach with which you will become familiar later is that you can "cross multiply." This means $(x)(4) = (3)(6)$. Then $4x = 18$, so $x = 4.5$.

Example: *What is the value of x in the equation $-\frac{2}{3}x = 12$?*

9

Solution: We recognize that $-\frac{2}{3}$ is multiplied by x. Therefore, we must

divide 12 by $-\frac{2}{3}$. This is the same as multiplying by $-\frac{3}{2}$. So,

$\left(-\frac{3}{2}\right)\left(-\frac{2}{3}x\right) = 1x$. Then $x = (12)\left(-\frac{3}{2}\right) = \frac{12}{1}\left(-\frac{3}{2}\right) = \frac{-36}{2} = -18$.

Example: *What is the value of x in the equation $\frac{4}{7}x = \frac{7}{12}$?*

10

Solution: Similar to Example 9, we note that x is multiplied by $\frac{4}{7}$. To solve the

equation, we must divide $\frac{7}{12}$ by $\frac{4}{7}$. This is equivalent to multiplying

by $\frac{7}{4}$. Then $\left(\frac{7}{4}\right)\left(\frac{4}{7}x\right) = \left(\frac{7}{4}\right)\left(\frac{7}{12}\right)$. Thus, $x = \frac{49}{48}$.

Example: *What is the value of x in the equation $9x = \frac{5}{3}$?*

11

Solution: Since x is multiplied by 9, we must divide $\frac{5}{3}$ by 9. $\frac{9x}{9} = \frac{5}{3} \div 9$. Then

$x = \frac{5}{3} \div 9 = \frac{5}{3} \times \frac{1}{9} = \frac{5}{27}$.

Example: *What is the value of x in the equation $-\frac{2}{9} + x = -\frac{2}{9}$?*

12

Solution: Since $\frac{2}{9}$ is already subtracted from x on the left side of the

equation, we must add $\frac{2}{9}$ to each side. $-\frac{2}{9} + x + \frac{2}{9} = -\frac{2}{9} + \frac{2}{9}$. Then,

$x = -\frac{2}{9} + \frac{2}{9} = 0$. This is really an answer! Zero is considered an

answer in the same way as any other number.

Each of these examples illustrates how to solve a one-step linear equation. Basically, you are "undoing" an operation that is already applied to the variable. Thus, if x is already added to a particular number, that number must be subtracted from each side of the equation. Also, if x is already multiplied by a particular number, we need to divide by that number on each side of the equation.

Note that dividing by a number such as $\frac{3}{4}$ really means multiplying by $\frac{4}{3}$.

Test Yourself!

Solve for the variable.

1. $x + 6 = -17$ *Answer:* _____

2. $\dfrac{y}{-4} = 20$ *Answer:* _____

3. $-5w = -65$ *Answer:* _____

4. $c - 3 = \dfrac{2}{3}$ *Answer:* _____

5. $p + \dfrac{3}{4} = \dfrac{9}{5}$ *Answer:* _____

6. $10k = 3$ *Answer:* _____

7. $\dfrac{3}{5}z = -30$ *Answer:* _____

8. $\dfrac{x}{12} = \dfrac{5}{8}$ *Answer:* _____

9. $5n = -\dfrac{3}{7}$ *Answer:* _____

10. $\dfrac{4}{9}m = \dfrac{2}{3}$ *Answer:* _____

Linear Equations in One Variable—Part 2

In this lesson, we will continue to explore the methods to solve a linear equation in one variable. The material you learned in Lesson 2 will be crucial to understanding the material in this lesson. The equations will need more than one step to solve, so be patient and careful. We will also study linear equations that have either no solution or infinitely many solutions. In this lesson, we will use different letters to represent the unknown quantity.

Your Goal: When you have completed this lesson, you should be able to solve any linear equation in one variable.

LESSON 3

Linear Equations in One Variable—Part 2

Before we begin solving the linear equations, let's talk about **like terms**. In general, terms involve a letter, number, or any combination of these connected by multiplication. Some examples of terms are 3, $-x$, $6y$, $5w^2$, and $\frac{3}{4}xy$. Remember that $-x = -1x$. Like terms (also called similar terms) are defined as algebraic expressions, involving one or more variables, in which there is an identical match with regard to exponents for each variable. The following examples are pairs of *similar terms* (like terms):

(a) $6x$ and $.05x$ (b) $-y^2$ and $50y^2$ (c) $16x^2z$ and $2.5x^2z$

The following examples are pairs of unlike terms. (These are <u>not</u> similar.)

(d) $2x$ and $\frac{1}{5}y$ (e) $4x$ and $11x^2$ (f) $4xy^2$ and $-4x^2y$

Note why example (f) does not have *like terms*. The exponents must match <u>exactly</u>.

When we combine *like terms* by addition or subtraction, we simply add (or subtract) the numbers preceding these terms. These numbers are called "coefficients."

1

Example: *What is the simplest way to write 6x + 0.05x?*

Solution: We just combine the coefficients (6 and 0.05) and leave the variable alone. The answer is $6.05x$.

2

Example: *What is the simplest expression for $-y^2 + 50y^2$?*

Solution: Recognizing that $-y^2 = -1y^2$, the answer is $49y^2$. Notice that we just calculated $-1 + 50$. The "y^2" gets attached to 49.

3

Example: *What is the simplest expression for $16x^2z - 2.5x^2z = ?$*

Solution: We just evaluate $16 - 2.5$, which is 13.5. As in the previous two examples, the "x^2z" gets attached to 13.5. The answer is $13.5x^2z$.

MathFlash!

Unlike terms cannot be added or subtracted. Do not try to combine into one term the examples shown below.

$$3x \text{ and } \frac{1}{4}y \qquad\qquad 9x \text{ and } 13x^2 \qquad\qquad 7xy^2 \text{ and } -7x^2y$$

The linear equations you are about to solve will involve at least two steps. Do you remember the order of operations?

If there are no parentheses or exponents, multiplication or division comes before addition or subtraction.

But, in solving linear equations involving any or all of these four basic operations, the procedure is reversed.

We **add or subtract before multiplying or dividing**. The answer you get can be checked for accuracy. We will show how this is done in a few examples.

4

Example: *What is the value of x in the equation $3x + 4 = 19$?*

Solution: The first step is to subtract 4 (add –4) to both sides of the equation.
We get $3x + 4 - 4 = 19 - 4$.
Then simplify this equation to $3x = 15$.
Finally, divide both sides by 3 to get $x = 5$.

To check that this answer is correct, substitute 5 for x in the original equation, so that it reads as $(3)(5) + 4 = 19$. $19 = 19$.
The answer of $x = 5$ is correct.

5

Example: *What is the value of y in the equation 6y – 13 = –16?*

Solution: The first step is to add 13 to both sides of the equation to get $6y - 13 + 13 = -16 + 13$. Then simplify to $6y = -3$. Finally, divide both sides by 6 to get $y = -\frac{3}{6}$, which reduces to $-\frac{1}{2}$. Note that the answer is <u>not</u> 2.

To check, substitute $-\frac{1}{2}$ for y wherever it appears in the equation: $(6)\left(-\frac{1}{2}\right) - 13 = -16$. You know that $(6)\left(-\frac{1}{2}\right) = -3$, so you can easily verify that $-3 - 13 = -16$.

MathFlash!

In the first step of each of these examples, we want to make sure that only the variable will appear on the left side.

6

Example: *What is the value of z in the equation $\frac{z}{9} - 2 = 7$?*

Solution: Add 2 to both sides of the equation, so it reads as $\frac{z}{9} - 2 + 2 = 7 + 2$. Simplifying this equation, we get $\frac{z}{9} = 9$. Finally, multiply both sides by 9 to get $z = (9)(9) = 81$.

7

Example: *What is the value of k in the equation $20 - \frac{k}{3} = 5$?*

Solution: First, we will subtract 20 from both sides of the equation to get $20 - \frac{k}{3} - 20 = 5 - 20$. Simplify to get $-\frac{k}{3} = -15$. Since k means $1k$, we can write $-\frac{k}{3} = -15$ as $\left(-\frac{1}{3}\right)(k) = -15$.

Finally, divide –15 by $-\frac{1}{3}$. Then $k = (-15) \div \left(-\frac{1}{3}\right) = (-15)(-3) = 45$.

8

Example: *What is the value of w in the equation* $4w - \dfrac{3}{2} = -\dfrac{5}{13}$ *?*

Solution: First multiply the entire equation by 26. This is the least common multiple (LCM) of the denominators of the given fractions. Now we have: $(26)(4w) - (26)\left(\dfrac{3}{2}\right) = (26)\left(-\dfrac{5}{13}\right)$. Simplify the equation to $104w - 39 = -10$. Add 39 to each side of the equation to get $104w = -10 + 39 = 29$.

Finally, dividing each side of the equation by 104, $\dfrac{104w}{104w} = \dfrac{29}{104}$.

So, $w = \dfrac{29}{104}$.

9

Example: *What is the value of c in the equation* $-\dfrac{5}{4} + \dfrac{c}{6} = -3$ *?*

Solution: The LCM of 4 and 6 is 12. Multiply the equation by 12 to get $(12)\left(-\dfrac{5}{4}\right) + (12)\dfrac{c}{6} = (12)(-3)$.

Before we do the next step, keep in mind that $\dfrac{c}{6}$ really means $\left(\dfrac{1}{6}\right)(c)$.

The next step is $-15 + 2c = -36$. Add 15 to both sides of the equation to get $2c = -21$. Finally, $c = -\dfrac{21}{2}$ or, equivalently, -10.5. To check yourself, substitute $c = -10.5$ into the original equation.

10

Example: *What is the value of v in the equation* $9v + 5v = -84$ *?*

Solution: At the beginning of this lesson, we spoke about combining like terms. Here we can combine $9v$ and $5v$ to get $14v$. Then $14v = -84$, which means that $v = \dfrac{-84}{14} = -6$.

Example: *What is the value of p in the equation* $-\frac{5}{3}p + p = -8$ *?*
11

Solution: You could multiply the entire equation by 3, but if you recognize that p means $1p$, we can simplify the left side by combining $-\frac{5}{3}p$ and $1p$. Since $-\frac{5}{3}p + 1p = -\frac{5}{3}p + \frac{3}{3}p = -\frac{2}{3}p$, we have $-\frac{2}{3}p = -8$.

Finally, divide -8 by $-\frac{2}{3}$, which means $(-8)\left(-\frac{3}{2}\right)$. Thus $p = 12$.

Let's check this answer. Once you calculate $\left(-\frac{5}{3}\right)(12)$ as -20, it should be easy to see that $-20 + 12 = -8$.

Example: *What is the value of m in the equation –4m + 22 = 6m +14?*
12

Solution: We want to "force" any expression with m to end up on the left side of the equation, and any number to end up on the right side of the equation. We don't want 22 on the left side, so subtract 22 from both sides. We get: $-4m - 22 + 22 = 6m + 14 - 22$. Simplify each side so that it reads as $-4m = 6m - 8$.

Now, we want to remove $6m$ from the right side, so we subtract $6m$ from each side: $-4m - 6m = 6m - 8 - 6m$. This simplifies to $-10m = -8$. Finally, we divide -8 by -10 to get the answer of $m = \frac{8}{10}$, which reduces to $\frac{4}{5}$, or the decimal equivalent of $\frac{8}{10}$ which is 0.8.

Example: *What is the value of t in the equation* $2t - \frac{4}{9} = 4t + \frac{3}{4}$*?*
13

Solution: Let's use the LCM of 9 and 4, which is 36, to remove the denominators. Then $(36)(2t) - (36)\left(\frac{4}{9}\right) = (36)(4t) + (36)\left(\frac{3}{4}\right)$.

Doing the multiplication, we get $72t - 16 = 144t + 27$. Let's subtract $144t$ from each side so that the equation reads as $72t - 16 - 144t = 144t + 27 - 144t$. Simplify to $-72t - 16 = 27$. Add 16 to both sides to get $-72t - 16 + 16 = 27 + 16$. Simplify to $-72t = 43$.

Finally, $t = -\frac{43}{72}$.

14

Example: *What is the value of w in the equation –6w + 3.6 = 9w –4.2?*

Solution: First subtract 9w on both sides of the equation, so that we have –6w + 3.6 – 9w = 9w – 4.2 – 9w. This simplifies to –15w + 3.6 = –4.2. Then subtract 3.6 from both sides of the equation to get –15w = –7.8. Finally, divide to get –7.8 by –15, w = 0.52.

We will end this lesson with an example showing no solution, an example showing an indefinite number of solutions (too many to count), and an example showing a solution of zero. Recall that zero counts as an answer; thus, zero does <u>not</u> mean "no solution."

15

Example: *What is the value of z in the equation 7z – 2 = 7z + 3?*

Solution: If you follow the procedure we have been using in the last few examples, you will eventually get the equation 0z = 5. The answer would be the value of $\frac{5}{0}$, which has no meaning. Thus, this equation has no solution.

16

Example: *What is the value of w in the equation 8w – 4 = –4 + 8w?*

Solution: By subtracting 8w from each side, the equation reads –4 = –4. Of course, this statement is always true. Our conclusion is that there are an indefinite number of solutions. (Another word for "indefinite" is "infinite.")

17

Example: *What is the value of k in the equation –5k + 11 = –8k + 11?*

Solution: First add 8k to both sides to get 3k + 11 = 11. Upon subtracting 11 from both sides, the equation will read 3k = 0. Finally, $k = \frac{0}{3} = 0$.

Test Yourself!

1. Which one of the following pairs represents like terms?

    (A) $-2y$ and $5y^2$ (C) wy and $3wy^2$

    (B) $9xz$ and $0.4xz$ (D) $0.8x$ and $0.8y$

2. Which one of the following equations has no solution?

    (A) $3t - 4 = -3t + 1$ (C) $5t + 4 = 4t + 5$

    (B) $4t - 7 = -7$ (D) $6t + 2 = 6t - 2$

For 3–10, solve for the variable.

3. $5x + 22 = -38$ Answer: _____

4. $\dfrac{k}{7} + 3 = 11$ Answer: _____

5. $\dfrac{w}{4} - \dfrac{2}{3} = 2$ Answer: _____

6. $10y - 6y = -25$ Answer: _____

7. $-\dfrac{7}{6}z + z = -12$ Answer: _____

8. $5n - 32 = 13n - 35$ Answer: _____

9. $6y + \dfrac{5}{6} = 3y - \dfrac{4}{15}$ Answer: _____

10. $-7c + 2.8 = -2c - 0.7$ Answer: _____

Linear Inequalities in One Variable

In this lesson, we will explore the methods used to solve a linear inequality in one variable. These methods will resemble those used in Lessons 2 and 3 very closely. Each inequality will have only one letter that represents the unknown quantity. The key difference will be in the representation of the answer. < (less than), > (greater than), symbols will be used instead of =.

Your Goal: When you have completed this lesson, you should be able to solve any linear inequality in one variable.

Linear Inequalities in One Variable

Before we can solve these inequalities, we must discuss the number line, which appears below.

Notice that the number line is indefinite in length, and for convenience, the number 0 is placed in the center. The positive numbers are to the right of zero. The negative numbers are to the left of zero. In comparing the size of any two numbers, the number that lies further to the right is the larger of the two. Likewise, if you are given any set of numbers, the smallest will lie furthest to the left.

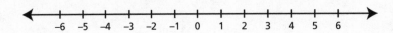

1

Example: *Given the numbers 6, $\frac{3}{2}$, −1, which number is smallest?*

Solution: Since any negative number is smaller than any positive number, the answer must be −1. It is the only number here that lies to the left of zero.

2

Example: *Given the numbers −4, $-\frac{7}{3}$, $-\frac{12}{5}$, −3, which number is largest?*

Solution: We already know that −3 is larger than −4, since −3 lies further to the right. Both $-\frac{7}{3}$ and $-\frac{12}{5}$ are between −3 and −2, so they would be larger than either −3 or −4. Computing the decimal equivalent, $-\frac{7}{3} = -2.\overline{3}$ and $-\frac{12}{5} = -2.4$. Since 2.4 is greater than 2.$\overline{3}$, we can conclude that −2.$\overline{3}$ is larger than −2.4. Our answer should be the number corresponding to − 2.$\overline{3}$, which is $-\frac{7}{3}$.

MathFlash!

When comparing two negative numbers, consider the corresponding positive numbers. The size of the numbers is reversed. For example, in comparing -4 and $-\dfrac{17}{4}$, you can look at 4 and $\dfrac{17}{4}$. Since $\dfrac{17}{4} = 4.25$, we know that $\dfrac{17}{4}$ is larger than 4. Therefore, -4 is larger than $-\dfrac{17}{4}$.

MathFlash!

The number zero has its place using the inequality symbols. We can write $0 > -6$ and $0 < 4\dfrac{2}{3}$. Remember that zero is always less than any positive number and is greater than any negative number.

3

Example: *What is the value of x in the inequality 5x < 30?*

Solution: We use practically the same methods as for equations. Just divide each side by 5 to get $x < 6$. Note that there is no one single value of x in the answer; there are an indefinite number of actual values, namely, any number less than 6. Here is the graphical representation of the answer: Zero is included simply as a reference number for all examples.

4

Example: *What is the value of z in the inequality 4z + 19 > 12?*

Solution: First subtract 19 from each side. This will yield $4z > -7$. Dividing each side by 4, we get $z > -\frac{7}{4}$. How this looks as a graph is shown below.

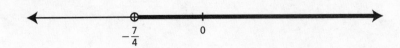

5

Example: *What is the value of y in the inequality 9y − 3 ≤ 5y − 23?*

Solution: The symbol ≤ means "less than or equal to."
Add 3 to each side to get $9y \le 5y - 20$.
Next, subtract 5y from each side to get $4y \le -20$.
Finally, divide each side by 4 to get the answer of $y \le -5$.
Here is how we graph it.

Let's Review
SEE LESSON **3**
Ex. 12-17

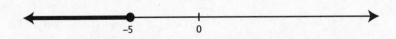

Given any inequality, whenever you multiply (or divide) each side by a negative number, the direction of the inequality sign changes. This will happen whether or not the original numbers are positive, negative, or zero.

> When $5 > 2$ is multiplied by −3, the correct inequality becomes $-15 < -6$.
> As another example, consider $-9 < 7$. Let's multiply each side by −2.
> Changing (correctly) the direction of the inequality sign, we get $18 > -14$.
>
> You should be able to conclude that the same phenomenon happens when an inequality is divided by a negative number. Let's start with $-10 > -20$. Dividing each side by −5 and changing the direction of the inequality sign, we get $2 < 4$.
>
> Let's not forget about the number zero. If the inequality were $0 < 8$ and we divided each side by −4 (and changed the direction of the inequality sign), we should get $0 > -2$.

6

Example: *What is the value of c in the inequality −3c − 10 < 38?*

Solution: First, add 10 to each side to get $-3c < 48$. Now, divide each side by −3 and change the direction of the inequality sign. Our answer is $c > -16$.

We graph it this way:

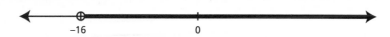

Example: *What is the value of w in the inequality –8w + 12 ≥ 16?*

7

Solution: First, subtract 12 from each side to get –8w ≥ 4. Now, we divide each side by –8 and change the direction of the inequality sign. Our answer is $w \le -\dfrac{1}{2}$. (Note that $-\dfrac{4}{8}$ was reduced to $-\dfrac{1}{2}$.) We graph it this way:

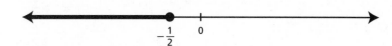

Example: *What is the value of x in the double inequality –5 < 7x + 16 < 16?*

8

Solution: Even though there are two inequality signs, we use the same rules as we did in the previous examples. First, subtract 16 from each "third" of this inequality to get –21 < 7x < 0. Now, divide every quantity by 7 to get –3 < x < 0. We graph it like this:

Example: *What is the value of g in the double inequality –20 < –6g + 13 ≤ 7?*

9

Solution: First, subtract 13 from all three parts of this inequality to get –33 < –6g ≤ –6. Finally, divide by –6 and remember to change the direction of the inequality. Our answer is $5\dfrac{1}{2} > g \ge 1$. We graph it like this:

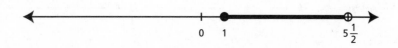

Example: *What is the value of p in the inequality $-\frac{2}{3}p + 5 < p + \frac{5}{4}$?*

10

Solution: The easiest way to solve this inequality is to multiply all four terms by the least common multiple, namely, 12. Then, the inequality will appear as $-8p + 60 < 12p + 15$. Subtract 60 from each side to get $-8p < 12p - 45$. Now, subtract 12p from each side to get $-20p < -45$. Now divide each side by −20 to get $p > \frac{-45}{-20}$. Then simplify $\frac{-45}{-20}$ to $\frac{9}{4}$. Finally, $p > \frac{9}{4}$. This is how we graph it:

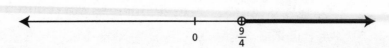

Test Yourself!

For 1–8, solve the inequality for the variable and graph it on the line provided to the right of the solution.

1. $11x < 6x < -10$ Answer: _____

   Graph: ←————————|————————→
                       0

2. $-3w + 19 > 1$ Answer: _____

   Graph: ←————————|————————→
                       0

3. $7z - 20 > 3z + 10$ Answer: _____

   Graph: ←————————|————————→
                       0

4. $\frac{3}{2}y - 4 < \frac{9}{5}y + 1$ Answer: _____

   Graph: ←————————|————————→
                       0

Test Yourself! (continued)

5. $x + 3.5 < 0.2x + 7.1$ Answer: _____

Graph: <———————————————|———————————————>
                                          0

6. $2k + \dfrac{1}{8} \geq \dfrac{5}{4}k - 1$ Answer: _____

Graph: <———————————————|———————————————>
                                          0

7. $12 > -5c - 18 \geq -23$ Answer: _____

Graph: <———————————————|———————————————>
                                          0

8. $2 > -4c - 18 > -20$ Answer: _____

Graph: <———————————————|———————————————>
                                          0

9.   **Which of the following is largest?** $-\dfrac{6}{5}, -1.3, -\dfrac{13}{12}, -1.29$

Answer: _____

10.   **If the numbers** $-0.85, -\dfrac{5}{6}, -0.8, -\dfrac{6}{7}, -\dfrac{15}{17}$ **were arranged in increasing order, which one would be the middle number?**

Answer: _____

Properties of Real Numbers

In this lesson, we will explore a few properties of real numbers. These properties will help us to solve additional linear equations in one variable, as well as more advanced equations. However, our equations in this lesson will still be linear with a single variable. Some of these properties will appear to be very easy, but they are very important to the understanding of more advanced topics.

Your Goal: When you have completed this lesson, you should have a sound understanding of these properties and be able to solve linear equations in which they are used. Although we will use integers in explaining these properties, we could also use numbers such as fractions and decimals.

LESSON 5

Properties of Real Numbers

Property 1: Associative Property of Addition

Given any group of numbers, the order in which you add them doesn't change the answer. This means that you can move the parentheses without changing the sum. Algebraically, given x, y, z, $(x + y) + z = x + (y + z)$.
Let $x = 3$, $y = 4$, and $z = 6$.
$(3 + 4) + 6 = 3 + (4 + 6)$. This is easy to check; $7 + 6 = 3 + 10$, so both sides equal 13.

Property 2: Associative Property of Multiplication

This property is very similar to Property 1; the only difference is that instead of using the addition operation for the three given numbers, we will use the multiplication operation. Given x, y, z, $(x \times y) \times z = x \times (y \times z)$.
Let $x = -2$, $y = 8$, and $z = 5$.
$[(-2) \times 8] \times 5 = (-2) \times (8 \times 5)$.
This equation simplifies to $(-16)(5) = (-2)(40)$. Both sides equal -80.

MathFlash!

$(x \times y) \times z$ and $(x) \times (y \times z)$ can each be written as xyz.

Property 3: Commutative Property of Addition

Given any two numbers to be summed, either one may appear first. The sum will be the same. Algebraically, given x and y, $x + y = y + x$.
Let $x = -1$ and $y = 7$.
$(-1) + 7 = 7 + (-1)$.
We can easily check that each side equals 6.

Property 4:   Commutative Property of Multiplication

This property is similar to Property 3. In this case, given x and y, $x \times y = y \times x$.
Sometimes, this property will appear with parentheses as $(x)(y) = (y)(x)$.
Let $x = 3$ and $y = 5$.
$(3)(5) = (5)(3)$. Of course, each side equals 15.

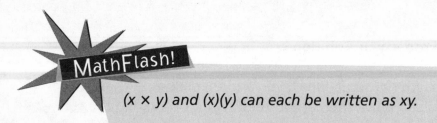

($x \times y$) and ($x)(y)$ can each be written as xy.

Property 5:   Distributive Property of Multiplication Over Addition

Multiplying a first number by the sum of two other numbers is the same as multiplying this first number by each of the other two numbers, then adding the products.

This property will be very useful in solving equations and inequalities that will soon follow. Algebraically, given x, y, z, $(x)(y + z) = (x)(y) + (x)(z)$. The right side of this equation is commonly written as $xy + xz$.
Let $x = 9$, $y = 4$, and $z = 10$.
Then, $(9)(4 + 10) = (9)(4) + (9)(10)$.
The left side has a value of $(9)(14) = 126$.
The right side has a value of $36 + 90$, which is also worth 126.

Although there is a more extensive list of number properties, these are the most commonly used. Always be careful that you <u>do not</u> calculate $(9)(4 + 10)$ as $9 \times 4 + 10$. The value of $(9)(4 + 10)$ is $(9)(4) + (9)(10) = 126$, whereas the value of $9 \times 4 + 10$ is only 46.

Property 5 can be used when any or all of x, y, and z are negative numbers. This means effectively that (x)(y − z) = xy − xz, since y − z is equivalent to y + (−z). Likewise, xy − xz is equivalent to xy + (−xz). For example (−5)[(−3) − (−1)] = (−5)(−3) − (−5)(−1). The left side becomes (−5)(−2) and the right side becomes 15 − 5. Both sides equal 10.

1

Example: *What is the value of x in the equation 3(x + 4) = 10?*

Solution: Since the number 3 is "attached" to the quantity (x + 4), we interpret this as a multiplication, such as 3x from our previous lessons. By Property 5, 3(x + 4) means the same as (3)(x) + (3)(4) = 3x + 12.
Thus, the equation becomes 3x + 12 = 10.
After subtracting 12 from each side, the equation simplifies to
3x = −2. Then $x = -\dfrac{2}{3}$.

2

Example: *What is the value of y in the equation 14 − 5(y + 2) = −36?*

Solution: Be extra careful here! Do not subtract 5 from 14. First we use Property 5 to rewrite the equation as 14 − 5y − 10 = −36. Notice we multiplied the −5 times the y and the 2. Make sure you understand why −10, not +10, is written. Next: 4 − 5y = −36. Subtract 4 from each side to get −5y = −40. Finally, y = 8.

3

Example: *What is the value of z in the equation 6(2 − z) = 4(z + 8)?*

Solution: Simplifying each side, we get 12 − 6z = 4z + 32. Subtracting 12 from each side yields −6z = 4z + 20. Now subtract 4z from each side to get −10z = 20. Finally, z = −2.

4

Example: *What is the value of w in the inequality –2(4 + 5w) < 22?*

Solution: Using Property 5, we can eliminate parentheses by multiplying –2 by 4 and 5w to get –8 – 10w < 22. Adding 8 to each side yields –10w < 30, so w > –3. (We will omit the graphical feature for these inequalities since you already mastered them in Lesson 4!)

5

Example: *What is the value of c in the inequality 7(2c – 3) – 9(c – 4) ≤ 9?*

Solution: Using Property 5 twice, and being careful to distribute the negative sign correctly, we get 14c –21 – 9c + 36 ≤ 9. Simplifying the left side of the equation leads to 5c + 15 ≤ 9. After subtracting 15, we get 5c ≤ –6. Thus, $c \le -\dfrac{6}{5}$.

6

Example: *What is the value of t in the inequality –2 < 4(1 – 3t) ≤ 64?*

Solution: This example will give us practice on a double inequality and Property 5. Using Property 5, we get –2 < 4 – 12t ≤ 64. Subtracting 4 from all three "parts" yields –6 < –12t ≤ 60. Now, dividing by –12 and changing the order of the inequality gives us the answer of $\dfrac{1}{2} > t \ge -5$. You may also write your answer as $-5 \le t < \dfrac{1}{2}$.

MathFlash!

It is possible that an example using the Distributive Property of Multiplication Over Addition will have no answer. 15(x + 5) = 3(5x –1) is such an example. However, there will be an answer for each of the drill exercises that follow.

Here is an interesting application of the Distributive Property of Multiplication Over Addition. Suppose that you can read 60 words per minute, but your friend can read only 40 words per minute. What is the total combined number of words that you and your friend can read in 5 minutes? One method to get the answer is to calculate separately the number of words that you read in 5 minutes and the same for your friend. This means (60)(5) + (40)(5) = 500 words.

A second method is to add the number of words both of you read in 1 minute, then multiply that result by 5. This means (5)(60 + 40), which is equivalent to (5)(100) = 500 words. The final answer is the same.

 Test Yourself!

1. Which one of the following illustrates the Associative Property of Multiplication?

    (A) 16 × 3 = 3 × 16

    (C) (12 × 5) × 2 = 12 × (5 × 2)

    (B) (10 + 7) + 4 = 10 + (7 + 4)

    (D) 11 + 9 = 9 + 11

2. Which one of the following illustrates the Commutative Property of Addition?

    (A) 13 + 7 = 7 + 13

    (C) (14 + 6) + 2 = 14 + (6 + 2)

    (B) 15 × 4 = 4 × 15

    (D) (18 × 3) × 7 = 18 × (3 × 7)

For 3–10, solve for the variable. Your answers for 7–10 must include the same number of inequality signs as given in the original inequality.

3. $6(5 - x) = 39$ *Answer:* _____

4. $20 - 3(3x + 13) = -73$ *Answer:* _____

5. $2(8y - 5) = -3(7 - 4y)$ *Answer:* _____

6. $y + 9(y - 20) = 0$ *Answer:* _____

Test Yourself! (continued)

7. $16(z + 3) < -24$ Answer: _____

8. $19 + 4(5z - 1) \geq 55$ Answer: _____

9. $3(9 + w) - 2(2w + 7) \leq -15$ Answer: _____

10. $-6 < 8(6 - w) < 80$ Answer: _____

LESSONS 1-5

QUIZ ONE

1. Consider the following list of numbers.
$$-4.12, \; -\frac{13}{3}, \; -4.\overline{1}, \; -4\frac{1}{4}, \; -4.3$$
Which one of the numbers is the largest?

   A $-\dfrac{13}{3}$

   B -4.12

   C $-4.\overline{1}$

   D $-4\dfrac{1}{4}$

2. If $w = \dfrac{2}{5}$, what is the value of $10w - \dfrac{20}{w} + 1$?

   A -45

   B -24

   C -18

   D -3

3. Which one of the following illustrates the Commutative Property of Multiplication?

   A $(2 \times 13) \times 7 = 2 \times (13 \times 7)$

   B $(13 + 7) + 2 = (7 + 13) + 2$

   C $2 + (7 + 13) = (2 + 7) + 13$

   D $(7 \times 2) \times 13 = (2 \times 7) \times 13$

4. If $y = -5$, what is the value of $4y - 3y^2$?

   A -95

   B -50

   C 10

   D 55

5. What is the value of k in the equation $\dfrac{5}{6} + k = 30$?

   A 25

   B $29\dfrac{1}{6}$

   C $30\dfrac{5}{6}$

   D 36

6. What are the values of z in the inequality $5 + 4(6 - z) > 28$?

   A $z < -4$

   B $z > 4$

   C $z < \dfrac{1}{4}$

   D $z > -\dfrac{1}{4}$

7. Which one of the following represents a pair of like terms?

   A $4xt$ and $16x^2t^2$

   B $8yw^2$ and $3w^2y$

   C $2wt$ and $2wy$

   D $10wyt$ and $-10wyt^2$

8. What are the values of c in the inequality $-32 < 5c + 8 < -12$?

   A $-8 < c < -4$

   B $-8 < c < 4$

   C $-\dfrac{24}{5} < c - \dfrac{4}{5}$

   D $-\dfrac{24}{5} < c < \dfrac{4}{5}$

9. **What is the value of *n* in the equation**
    $10n - \dfrac{3}{4} = n - \dfrac{1}{8}$?

    A $\dfrac{25}{4}$

    B $\dfrac{45}{8}$

    C $\dfrac{7}{80}$

    D $\dfrac{5}{72}$

10. **Which one of the following equations has an answer of zero?**

    A $9x = -9$

    B $x + \dfrac{1}{9} = \dfrac{1}{9}$

    C $\dfrac{1}{9}x = \dfrac{1}{9}$

    D $x - 9 = 9$

Word Problem Applications for Equations in One Variable

In this lesson, we will explore a few types of word problems that use the techniques you learned to solve a linear equation in one variable. Here are a few suggestions that will help you succeed in writing the correct algebraic equation for a given word problem.

1. Read the problem carefully in order to understand exactly what information is given and what information is requested.

2. Use a picture or a chart, if possible, that shows the given information.

3. Identify the unknown quantity by assigning a variable, such as *x*, to it.

4. Translate the words of the problem into an equation that uses the unknown quantity.

5. Solve the equation and state the answer with the appropriate units, if applicable. (Example: inches, minutes, pounds, etc.)

6. Be sure your answer seems reasonable. Then check it for accuracy.

Your Goal: When you have completed this lesson, you should be able to solve several types of word problems that involve the use of a single variable.

LESSON 6

Word Problem Applications for Equations in One Variable

Example:

Marlene wishes to put all her paper clips into two boxes. She has a total of 70 paper clips. The second box will contain 20 more paper clips than the first box.
How many paper clips will she put into the first box?

Solution:

Let x represent the number of paper clips in the first box. Can you think of the expression we should use to represent the number of paper clips in the second box? We need to show that the sum of the paper clips in the two boxes is 70. The second box must contain the difference of 70 and the number of paper clips in the first box: $70 - x$.

Next, we must use the fact that the second box has 20 more paper clips than the first box. We need to add 20 to the number of paper clips in the first box. In that way, the representation of the number of paper clips will be equal in the two boxes. Since $x + 20$ is the expression for "20 more than x," we write $x + 20 = 70 - x$.

Solving this equation is the easiest part! The equation will simplify to $2x = 50$, so the answer is $x = 25$. Thus, Marlene should place 25 paper clips into the first box.

Although not required, note that the second box must contain 25 + 20 = 45 paper clips. This verifies that the two boxes contain a total of 70 paper clips.

Example:

2

Henry has 32 dimes in his collection of dimes and nickels. The total value of his collection is $5.55. How many nickels does he have?

Solution: Let x represent the number of nickels. The total amount of $5.55 is composed of the value of the dimes added to the value of the nickels. The value of the dimes is (32)($0.10) = $3.20; the value of the nickels is 0.05x$. The equation becomes $3.20 + 0.05x$ = $5.55. For the purpose of solving, we can remove the dollar signs. Then the equation reduces to $0.05x = 2.35$, so the answer is $x = 47$ nickels.

To check: 47 nickels are equal to $2.35; the dimes equal $3.20; the total becomes $5.55.

Example:

3

Lynn has scored 87, 73, and 81 on her first three English exams. There will be one more exam next week. Lynn wants to achieve an average of 84 for all four exams. What score must she get on her exam next week?

Solution: Let x represent her fourth score. An average of 84 for four scores means their sum divided by 4 will equal 84. Algebraically, we could write $\dfrac{87 + 73 + 81 + x}{4} = 84$. This equation simplifies to $\dfrac{241 + x}{4} = 84$. The quickest way to solve this equation is to multiply both sides by 4. The left side becomes $241 + x$, and the right side becomes (84)(4) = 336. Thus, $241 + x = 336$, so $x = 95$.

You can easily check the validity of this answer by simply adding all four scores and dividing by 4.

Example: *Peter has just started a part-time job in which he is paid an hourly wage for every hour up through 35 hours. For each hour after 35 hours, he gets paid 50% higher than his hourly wage. Unfortunately, Peter forgot to ask his boss what hourly wage he will earn! For his first week, his gross (total) pay was $500.50 for a total of 42 hours.*
What is Peter's regular hourly wage?

4

Solution: Let x represent Peter's hourly wage. In order to represent his "bonus" hourly wage, for hours worked beyond 35, we must use an expression that represents "50% higher than x." 50% higher than any number is equivalent to multiplying that number by 1.50 or 1.5. Thus, Peter's "bonus" hourly wage is $1.5x$. His wages for the first 35 hours would be $35x$ dollars.

Since he worked a total of 42 hours, we know that he worked 7 hours at the "bonus" hourly wage of $1.5x$ dollars.
So, during the 7 additional hours he worked, his wages were $(7)(1.5x) = 10.5x$. Use the equation $35x + 10.5x = 500.50$
As in Example 2, the dollar signs may be dropped. This equation simplifies to $45.5x = 500.50$, so $x = \$11$ per hour.

In order to check this answer, we should first calculate his "bonus" hourly pay, which is $(\$11)(1.5) = \$16.50$. So, his cumulative gross pay must be $(\$11)(35) + (\$16.50)(7) = \$500.50$.

Example: *Diane is planning on driving from Pittsburgh to Louisville, a total of 420 miles. It takes her 4 hours to cover the first 200 miles. For the remainder of the trip, she can only average 40 miles per hour. Assume that there are no stops during this trip.*
How many hours will the entire trip take?

5

Solution: First, we must recognize that Rate × Time = Distance.
Let x represent the number of hours needed for the second part of the trip. Since she has already covered 200 miles, the unknown x refers only to the remaining 220 miles. Using an average (rate) of 40 miles per hour, the equation for the second part of the trip becomes $40x = 220$, so $x = 5.5$ hours. Don't stop here.

Remember that the question asked for the time for the <u>entire</u> trip. The first half of the trip took 4 hours, so the entire trip took $4 + 5.5 = 9.5$ hours.

6

Example: *At the local movie theater, tickets for children cost $2.50 apiece, whereas tickets for adults cost $6.00 apiece. Last Saturday, there were 24 more children than adults in the theater.*
The total amount of money collected from everyone was $604. How many adults were in the theater?

Solution: Let x represent the number of adults. Since there were 24 more children than adults, we'll use $x + 24$ for the number of children. The total amount paid by all adults is $6x$, and the total amount paid by all children is $(2.50)(x + 24)$. Since $604.00 was the total amount paid by everyone, $6x + (2.50)(x + 24) = 604$ is the equation we must solve. Note that the dollar signs are dropped. Using the Distributive Property, the equation becomes $6x + 2.50x + 60 = 604$. Then $8.50x + 60 = 604$, followed by $8.50x = 544$. Finally, $x = 64$ adults.

In order to check this answer, we first note that there must be $64 + 24 = 88$ children. The total amount of money collected from everyone must be $(88)(\$2.50) + (64)(\$6.00) = \$604$.

Before we do Example 7, let's introduce the concept of a deductible, as it is used in dental insurance. A deductible represents a portion of the cost to the individual. Since visits to dentists can be very expensive, insurance companies often require deductibles for individuals who choose an insurance plan. This deductible is normally part of the total amount owed for the actual dental work. After the deductible is reached, the insurance company will usually pay a majority (sometimes as high as 90%) of the remainder of the amount that is owed. Let's plug in some numbers to see how this works:

Susan has a dental insurance plan for which she has a $300 deductible. Her plan will pay 80% of any amount above $300. This means that Susan will pay the first $300 of her bill. Then, she will pay 20% of the balance of her bill. (Since the insurance company pays 80% of any amount in excess of $300, Susan pays 100% – 80% = 20%.) Let's suppose that she needs dental work that will cost $1000. She will pay $300, the insurance company will pay 80% of the balance of $700. Susan will still be responsible for 20% of this $700, which is $(0.20)(\$700) = \$140$. Thus, Susan will pay a total of $300 + $140 = $440.

As a check, note that the insurance company is responsible for paying $(0.80)(\$700) = \$560$. So, the $560 that the insurance company pays added to the $440 that Susan pays will equal $1000. This calculation will work for any example in which a person is responsible for a deductible and a second party (usually an insurance company) is responsible for a fixed percent of the balance of the total amount.

Example:

7

Tom has a dental insurance plan in which he has a $250 deductible. His insurance company will pay 90% of any amount in excess of $250. Recently, Tom had root canal work done. He cannot recall how much the total amount of the bill was, but he remembers that he paid a total of $465.
What was the total amount of the bill?

Solution:

Let x represent the total amount of the bill. After Tom pays his $250 deductible, he must pay 10% (100% – 90%) of the remaining amount, which can be represented by $x - 250$ dollars. Then Tom will have to pay $250 + (0.10)(x - 250)$ dollars. Dropping the dollar signs, we can write $250 + (0.10)(x - 250) = 465$.
This equation simplifies to $250 + 0.10x - 25 = 465$.
Further simplification yields $0.10x = 240$, so $x = \$2400$.

MathFlash!

To check this answer, we know that Tom first pays $250. Then the balance of the bill is $2150. He must pay 10% of $2150, which is $215. Finally, $250 + $215 = $465. If you were asked how much the insurance company had to pay, you could simply subtract $465 from $2400 to get $1935. Another method would be to take 90% of $2150, which is also $1935.

Example:

8

Deductibles can be applied to homeowners insurance in the same way as shown with dental insurance. Suppose Cheryl has a home insurance policy that includes flood insurance. Last week, her home suffered flood damage for which her insurance company paid $2295. Her policy states that she has a $500 deductible and that the insurance company will pay 85% of any amount in excess of $500. What was the actual total amount of the flood damage?

Solution:

Let x represent the total amount of flood damage. We need to write an equation in which the $2295 can be used. This amount would represent 85% of x – $500, <u>not</u> of x dollars. Remember that the insurance company does not pay for the first $500 worth of damage; that is Cheryl's responsibility. The appropriate equation is $2295 = (0.85)(x - 500)$, after dropping the dollar signs. This equation simplifies to $2295 = 0.85x - 425$. Then, $2720 = 0.85x$. Thus, $x = \$3200$.

MathFlash!

To check this answer, we first deduct Cheryl's deductible of $500 from $3200, which is $2700. The insurance company is obligated to pay 85% of $2700, which is (0.85)($2700) = $2295. If you were asked the amount that Cheryl had to pay, you could simply calculate $3200 – $2295 = $905.

Example: *At the VWX company, every employee is about to receive a 7% increase in salary. Nancy is an employee in this company and has calculated her increased annual salary to be $51,895.*
What was her annual salary before the increase?

9

Solution: Let x represent Nancy's annual salary before the increase. The amount of dollars in her increase can be represented by $0.07x$, which means that her new annual salary is represented by $x + 0.07x = 1.07x$. Then $1.07x = \$51,895$. Thus, $x = \$48,500$.

This answer should be very easy to check. Nancy's increase in salary is ($48,500)(0.07) = $3395. Now add $3395 to $48,500 to get $51,895. <u>Caution:</u> Be sure that you <u>do not</u> take 7% of $51,895. The percent change is based on her <u>original</u> salary, not on her new salary.

Example: *At the Shopwell department store, every item has been reduced by 25%. Taking advantage of this sale, Chris just paid $345 for a stove.*
How much money did he save?

10

Solution: One quick way to solve this example is to let x represent the amount of money Chris would have paid if there were no reduction. Then Chris's payment of $345 represents 100% – 25% = 75% of the original price. Then $0.75x = \$345$, which means that $x = \$460$.

Don't stop now! The question asked us how much money Chris <u>saved</u>. The correct answer is $460 – $345 = $115.

MathFlash!

In Example 10, if you had wanted x to represent the money he saved, then $345 + x would represent the original price of the stove. The $345 he paid would then represent 75% of $345 + x. So you could use the equation 345 = (0.75)(345 + x). If you solve this equation correctly, you will get x = $115.

Test Yourself!

Write an appropriate equation using *x* and solve for the unknown quantity.

1. Freddie has a total of 100 baseball cards in his collection. There are 36 more cards of National League players than there are of American League players. How many cards containing American League players does Freddie have?

    Equation: _____   *Answer:* _____

2. Viola has a part-time job in which she is paid on an hourly basis for every hour up through 40 hours. For each hour after 40 hours, she gets paid 60% higher than her hourly wage. This past week, she earned a total of $644.80 for working 46 hours. What is Viola's regular hourly wage?

    Equation: _____   *Answer:* _____

3. George intends to drive from Atlanta to Chicago, a distance of 710 miles. He drives at an average rate of 46 miles per hour for the first 5 hours. What is his average driving rate for the remainder of the trip if the entire trip takes 12.5 hours?

    Equation: _____   *Answer:* _____

4. At a local department store, the price of each item has been increased by 20%. Selma has just purchased a television for $432. How much would she have paid before the price increase?

    Equation: _____   *Answer:* _____

5. David has a dental insurance plan in which he has a $400 deductible. His insurance company will pay 70% of any amount in excess of $400. Recently, he had crowns placed on two teeth. David had to pay a total of $1090. What was the total amount of the bill?

    Equation: _____   *Answer:* _____

6. Cheyenne has 48 quarters in her collection of dimes and quarters. The total value of her collection is $16.20. How many dimes does she have?

    Equation: _____   *Answer:* _____

7. Miranda is a sales representative for a book publisher. Over each of the past four weeks, she has sold 65, 81, 46, and 50 books, respectively. She hopes that she can sell an average of 70 books for the current five-week period. How many books must Miranda sell this week to do that?

    Equation: _____   *Answer:* _____

8. At a large school concert, tickets for students are $1.50 apiece, whereas tickets for adults are $5.00 apiece. There are four times as many students as adults, and a total of $572.00 is collected. How many adults are attending the concert?

    Equation: _____   *Answer:* _____

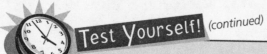

9.   At the WXYZ company, some layoffs have begun. For the remaining employees, there will be a 12% decrease in annual salary. Leo is one of the lucky employees who will not be laid off. After the salary decrease takes effect, his annual salary will be $33,792. What is Leo's current annual salary?

     Equation: _____   Answer: _____

10.   Phyllis has an auto insurance plan that pays 95% of any amount over her deductible, in case of an accident. Unfortunately, Phyllis's deductible is $1200. Last month, Phyllis was involved in an auto accident. The insurance company had to pay only $342. What was the total amount of money that Phyllis paid?

     Equation: _____   Answer: _____

Word Problem Applications for Inequalities in One Variable

In this lesson, we will look at a few types of word problems that use the techniques you learned to solve a linear inequality in one variable. You might want to review the suggestions given at the beginning of Lesson 6, since they will help you in this lesson. Lesson 7 problems will be similar to those of Lesson 6, but keep in mind that each answer will be written as an inequality. As before, be sure that your answer seems reasonable.

Your Goal: When you have completed this lesson, you should be able to solve several types of word problems dealing with inequalities that use a single variable.

LESSON 7

Word Problem Applications for Inequalities in One Variable

Example: *Megan is buying turkey and roast beef for a large party she is hosting. The cost of turkey is $6.25 per pound, and the cost of roast beef is $8.50 per pound. Each of these meats is sold only in whole numbers of pounds. She has a maximum of $150 to spend, and she has already decided to buy 12 pounds of turkey. What is the maximum number of pounds of roast beef that Megan can buy?*

Solution: Let x represent the number of pounds of roast beef. The 12 pounds of turkey will cost $(12)(\$6.25) = \$75.00$, and the x pounds of roast beef will cost $\$8.50x$. Since Megan cannot spend more than $150, the correct inequality is $75 + 8.50x \leq 75$. (The dollar signs can be dropped.) Simplify to $8.50x \leq 75$, so $x \leq 8.82$ pounds (rounded off). Since she cannot buy a fraction of a pound, we round <u>down</u> to 8 pounds.

MathFlash!

Quite often, in examples such as these, there will be a "leftover" when we check the answer. You will also observe that rounding up or down will be necessary in examples where only whole numbers are acceptable. To check the answer of Example 1, let's calculate the cost of 12 pounds of turkey and 8 pounds of roast beef. The total cost would be $(12)(\$6.25) + (8)(\$8.50) = \$143.00$.
Notice that Megan will have $7.00 left over, which is not enough to buy another pound of roast beef. This confirms that our answer is correct.

Example: *Jerry is buying shirts and suits at a clothing store. The store owner mentions that any customer who purchases at least $1000 worth of shirts and suits is entitled to a free weekend stay at the Holly Bay Inn. All shirts sell for $30 apiece, and all suits sell for $180 apiece. Jerry has already selected 3 suits to buy.*
What is the minimum number of shirts he must buy in order to get the free weekend at the Holly Bay Inn?

2

Solution: Let x represent the minimum number of shirts Jerry will buy. We know that he has already spent (3)($180) = $540 for the suits. The amount he will spend for the shirts is 30x$. Dropping the dollar signs, the correct inequality is $540 + 30x \geq 1000$. Simplify to $30x \geq 460$, so $x \geq 15\frac{1}{3}$ shirts.

Since <u>only a whole number of shirts can be bought</u>, we must round <u>up</u> to 16 shirts. As in Example 1, the traditional rounding rule is not used.

MathFlash!

To check our answer, the total cost of 3 suits and 16 shirts is (3)($180) + (16)($30) = $1020, so Jerry is entitled to his free getaway!
Note that if he had only bought 15 shirts, he would have spent a total of $990 and would not be eligible for the free getaway.

Example: *The manufacturer of a new car called the Pluto is claiming that this car can average at least 35 miles per gallon of gas. Paula has bought the Pluto, and after driving a distance of 100 miles, 4 gallons of gas has been used. She fills up her car with an additional 10 gallons of gas.*
If she does not fill up her car for the rest of her trip, what is the minimum whole number of additional miles Paula must travel in order to validate the claim of the manufacturer?

Solution: Let x represent the additional miles of travel. The miles per gallon figure is equal to the total miles divided by the number of gallons of gas. Paula's total distance is represented by $100 + x$. Since the total number of gallons of gas is 14, the correct inequality is $\dfrac{100 + x}{14} \geq 35$. By multiplying both sides by 14, this inequality simplifies to $100 + x \geq 490$, so $x \geq 390$ miles.

Notice that since the right side is already a whole number, there is no rounding off necessary for this example.

Example: *Ted wants to buy three-cent stamps and seven-cent stamps for his stamp collection. He can spend no more than $14 for these stamps. He has decided to buy 160 three-cent stamps.*
What is the maximum number of seven-cent stamps that Ted can buy?

Solution: Let x represent the number of seven-cent stamps. Ted will spend $(160)(\$0.03) = \$4.80$ on the three-cent stamps, so the correct inequality, without the dollar signs, is $4.80 + 0.07x \leq 14$. This simplifies to $0.07x \leq 9.20$, so $x \leq 131.43$ (rounded off). Since only whole numbers of stamps can be bought, the answer becomes 131 seven-cent stamps.

As a check, notice that $(160)(\$0.03) + (131)(\$0.07) = \$13.97$, which does not exceed $14. If Ted bought even one more seven-cent stamp, the total cost would exceed $14.

MathFlash!

For inequalities in which only whole numbers can represent solutions, remember to round <u>down</u> when the inequality is ≤ and round <u>up</u> when the inequality is ≥. Thus, if you wanted a <u>maximum</u> x value for either x ≤ 7.4 or x ≤ 7.9, the correct answer is 7. Similarly, if you wanted a <u>minimum</u> x value for either x ≥ 7.4 or x ≥ 7.9, the correct answer is 8.

Example: **The Arithmetic Toy Company plans on making a new multicolored calculator. The company will have fixed costs totaling $100,000 plus $35 for each calculator that it sells. The calculators will sell for $48 apiece.**
What is the minimum number of calculators that must be sold in order for the company to make a profit?

5

Solution: Let x represent the minimum number of calculators. In order to make a profit, the sales of the calculators must exceed the cost to make them. Then $48x$ represents the sales, and $100,000 + 35x$ represents the cost.

Notice that 100,000 is <u>not</u> multiplied by the number of calculators made, because this amount of money is a fixed cost. That is, the company would still incur this cost regardless of the number of calculators sold.
The desired inequality would be $48x > 100,000 + 35x$. This can be simplified to $13x > 100,000$. Thus, $x > 7692.31$.
This means that 7693 is the minimum number of calculators that must be sold so that the company makes a profit.

MathFlash!

Returning to Example 5, let's suppose that the fixed costs were $100,100. If everything else remained the same, the inequality would be $48x > 100,100 + 35x$. The solution would read $x > 7700$. Hopefully, you would realize that the minimum number of calculators that must be sold would be 7701, <u>not</u> 7700. If the company made 7700 calculators, there would be neither a profit nor a loss.

Example:

6

Janice is following a special diet in which her maximum weekly calories should not be more than 13,500. The total calories for all her main meals and drinks will be 11,000. The remaining calories will be for her desserts.
What is Janice's maximum allowable average whole number of calories per day for desserts? (Assume a full 7-day week.)

Solution:

Let x represent her maximum allowable average number of calories per day for desserts. Since $7x$ will represent her total maximum calories for desserts for the week, the correct inequality is $7x + 11{,}000 \leq 13{,}500$. Simplify to $7x \leq 2{,}500$. Then $x \leq 357.14$.

This means that 357 is the maximum average number of calories per day that Janice is allowed for desserts. (The good news is that she can still have a moderate portion of ice cream each day!)

Example:

7

Francine is undertaking a major research project. Her company is giving her two payment options. Her first option would be a flat fee of $4950 plus $40 per hour. Her second option would be no flat fee, but an hourly rate of $55 per hour. Francine would really prefer the second option.
What would be the minimum number of hours required so that the second option would be the more profitable for her?

Solution:

Let x represent the number of hours she works on this project. Her payment under the first option would be $4950 + 40x$ dollars, and her payment under the second option would be $55x$ dollars. Since Francine has chosen the second option, we want $55x > 4950 + 40x$. Then, we simplify this inequality to $15x > 4950$. So, $x > 330$. Our conclusion is that Francine must work at least 331 hours.

(Note that if she works 330 hours, she would get the same pay, namely, $18,150, under either option.)

Example: *In the town of Tinyville, there are two taxi companies. Company A charges a rider a flat rate of $5.00 plus $0.75 per mile. Company B charges a rider a flat rate of $7.50 plus $0.66 per mile. Sandra wishes to use the services of Company A.*
What is the maximum number of miles that she can travel in order for the total cost for a ride with Company A to be cheaper than with Company B?

Solution: Let x represent the maximum number of miles. The total cost using Company A is $5 + 0.75x$ dollars, and the total cost using Company B is $7.50 + 0.66x$. The desired inequality is $5 + 0.75x < 7.50 + 0.66x$, since we want the cost for using Company A to be less than the cost for Company B. Simplify this inequality, to get $0.75x < 2.50 + 0.66x$, then $0.99x < 2.50$, and finally $x < 27.\overline{7}$.

Thus, the maximum number of miles that Sandra can save money using Company A is 27. Incidentally, make sure you could calculate the actual cost for going 27 miles with both taxi companies ($25.25 with Company A vs. $25.32 with Company B).

Test Yourself!

Write an appropriate inequality using x and solve for the unknown quantity.

1.   The Geometric Gadget Company is developing a new math game. The company will have fixed costs totaling $120,000 plus $12 for each game that it sells. Each game will sell for $28.
What is the minimum number of math games that the company must sell in order to make a profit?

Equation: _____   Answer: _____

2.   Brad is on a strict diet. His doctor has ordered him to limit his average daily calorie intake to no more than 1200 over the next 14 days. Brad has ordered special meals, with no desserts, which will total 15,000 calories. The remaining calories can be used for chocolate pudding.
What is Brad's maximum allowable average whole number of calories per day for chocolate pudding?

Equation: _____   Answer: _____

Test Yourself! (continued)

3.   Nadine is a stamp collector. She wants to buy eight-cent stamps and eleven-cent stamps. She has decided to buy 120 eight-cent stamps. She will spend no more than $17.00 for all stamps.
     What is the maximum number of eleven-cent stamps that Nadine can buy?

     Equation: _____   *Answer:* _____

4.   Membership to the Solid Body Health Club can be accomplished in one of two ways. Option 1 requires an initial payment of $300 plus $9 per visit. Option 2 requires no initial payment but costs $15 per visit. Suzanne has decided to join this health club, using Option 1.
     What is the minimum number of visits she must make in order for this option to be the more economical of the two options?

     Equation: _____   *Answer:* _____

5.   Ben is buying hot dogs and hamburgers for a party. Each hot dog costs $1.40 and each hamburger costs $2.20. He will spend a maximum of $60. Ben decides to buy 21 hot dogs.
     What is the maximum number of hamburgers he can buy?

     Equation: _____   *Answer:* _____

6.   Kathleen has just been promoted to Vice President of Sales in her company. She has been offered a choice of two compensation packages. In Package #1, she would receive an annual salary of $170,000, plus 8% of all sales. In Package #2, she would get an annual salary of $115,000, plus 14% of all sales. Since Kathleen believes that her leadership will create many sales dollars, she has chosen Package #2.
     What is the minimum amount of sales dollars (in whole numbers of dollars) needed in order for Package #2 to be the better choice?

     Equation: _____   *Answer:* _____

7. In the village of Greenville, there are two limousine companies. Company X charges a flat rate of $55 plus $2.50 per mile. Company Y charges a flat rate of $80 plus $1.75 per mile. Trevor would prefer to use Company Y.
    What is the minimum number of miles he must travel in order for the total cost to be less than that of Company X?

    Equation: _____   *Answer:* _____

8. A freight elevator can hold a maximum of 1600 pounds. Jim and Joyce are placing chairs on this elevator. Jim weighs 170 pounds and Joyce weighs 106 pounds. Each chair weighs 17 pounds, in addition to Jim's and Joyce's weight.
    What is the maximum number of chairs that can be placed in this elevator?

    Equation: _____   *Answer:* _____

Proportions

In this lesson, we will explore proportions, which are defined as equal ratios. An example of a proportion would be $\frac{1}{3} = \frac{4}{12}$. A practical application of proportions would be comparing actual distances between two cities and their distances on a map. Suppose the legend of a map states that 1 inch represents a distance of 50 miles. If the actual distance between Harrisburg and Pittsburgh is 200 miles, then we would expect that the distance between them on a map would be 4 inches. We note that $\frac{50}{200} = \frac{1}{4}$.

Your Goal: When you have completed this lesson, you should be able to verify if two given ratios represent a proportion, as well as solve for a missing variable in any proportion.

LESSON

8

Proportions

Here are some examples of proportions:

(a) $\dfrac{2}{3} = \dfrac{6}{9}$ (b) $\dfrac{8}{18} = \dfrac{12}{27}$ (c) $\dfrac{7}{1} = \dfrac{28}{4}$ (d) $\dfrac{\frac{1}{2}}{5} = \dfrac{2}{20}$ (e) $\dfrac{\frac{1}{4}}{\frac{5}{8}} = \dfrac{0.6}{1.5}$

Let's discuss each of these.

    (a) The numerator and denominator of $\dfrac{6}{9}$ can be divided by 3 to yield $\dfrac{2}{3}$.

    (b) Each fraction can be reduced to $\dfrac{4}{9}$.

    (c) 28 divided by 4 is 7, which is $\dfrac{7}{1}$.

    (d) We can simplify to $\dfrac{\frac{1}{2}}{5}$, which means $\dfrac{1}{2} \times \dfrac{1}{5} = \dfrac{1}{10}$. Of course, $\dfrac{2}{20}$ reduces to $\dfrac{1}{10}$.

    (e) Looks imposing, but we can manage it! $\dfrac{\frac{1}{4}}{\frac{5}{8}}$ means $\dfrac{1}{4} \times \dfrac{8}{5} = \dfrac{8}{20} = \dfrac{2}{5}$.

For $\dfrac{0.6}{1.5}$, multiplying both numerator and denominator by 10, the fraction becomes $\dfrac{6}{15}$, which reduces to $\dfrac{2}{5}$.

You must be wondering if there is a quicker way to verify that each of these is a proportion. The good news is that there really is a simple procedure, which is to "cross-multiply."

    (a) Check that (2)(9) = (3)(6); both products are 18, so we have a match.

    (b) (8)(27) = 216, which is also the value of (12)(18).

    (c) (7)(4) = (28)(1) for sure.

    (d) $\left(\dfrac{1}{2}\right)(20) = 10$, which is certainly (2)(5).

    (e) Finally $\left(\dfrac{1}{4}\right)(1.5) = \dfrac{1.5}{4} = 0.375$, and $(0.6)\left(\dfrac{5}{8}\right)(0.625) = 0.375$.

Of course, the nature of algebra is that there is usually a missing element (also known as a variable) in equations or word problems, and the topic on proportions is no exception. Consider the following examples:

1

Example: *What is the value of x in $\frac{4}{11} = \frac{16}{x}$?*

Solution: By cross-multiplying, we get $4x = (16)(11) = 176$, $\frac{4x}{4} = \frac{176}{4}$, which leads to $x = 44$.

2

Example: *What is the value of x in $\frac{x}{1.4} = \frac{3}{0.2}$?*

Solution: By cross-multiplying, we get $0.2x = (1.4)(3) = 4.2$, $\frac{0.2x}{0.2} = \frac{4.2}{0.2}$, so $x = 21$.

3

Example: *What is the value of x in $\frac{2.5}{9} = \frac{x}{0.3}$?*

Solution: By cross-multiplying, we get $0.9x = 0.75$, and your answer would be $x = 0.08\overline{3}$.
In cases such as this, an answer such as 0.083 would also be considered sufficiently accurate.

MathFlash!

A good rule of thumb is to try to include at least two nonzero digits to the right of any decimal point for answers that contain at least the hundredths place. Thus, if you had an answer of 6.8264, you could generally leave the answer as 6.83. Likewise, an answer of 0.00543219 could be left as 0.0054.
For repeating decimals, the reader normally finds the use of the "bar" notation easier, as you saw in Example 3. (For instance, $0.08\overline{3}$ instead of 0.08333...)

Example:

4

What is the value of x in $\frac{x}{\frac{3}{5}} = \frac{2}{7}$?

Solution: By cross-multiplying, we get $7x = \left(\frac{3}{5}\right)(2) = \frac{6}{5}$. Then

$x = \left(\frac{6}{5}\right)\left(\frac{1}{7}\right) = \frac{6}{35}$. Note that if you changed $\frac{6}{5}$ to 1.2, your answer

would be 1.2 divided by 7, which is approximately 0.17.

Either answer should be acceptable.

Example:

5

What is the value of x in $\frac{\frac{3}{7}}{x} = \frac{\frac{9}{8}}{\frac{7}{4}}$?

Solution: Don't lose your concentration! By cross-multiplying (carefully), we

get $\left(\frac{9}{8}\right)x = \left(\frac{3}{7}\right)\left(\frac{7}{4}\right) = \frac{3}{4}$. Then $x = \frac{3}{4} \div \frac{9}{8} = \left(\frac{3}{4}\right)\left(\frac{8}{9}\right) = \frac{24}{36} = \frac{2}{3}$.

Example:

6

What is the value of x in $\frac{x}{4} = \frac{16}{\frac{5}{8}}$?

Solution: A word of caution! Do <u>not</u> divide 4 into 16. Remember to just cross-

multiply. We get $\left(\frac{5}{8}\right)x = 64$. Then $x = 64 \div \frac{5}{8} = (64)\left(\frac{8}{5}\right) = \frac{512}{5}$.

This answer would be acceptable, and so would $102\frac{2}{5}$ or 102.4.

Example:

7

What is the value of x in $\frac{x-2}{5} = \frac{x}{8}$?

Solution: Our first step would appear as $5x = 8(x - 2)$. We can simplify the
right side of this equation by using the Distributive Property of
Multiplication Over Addition (which also applies to subtraction,
since subtraction simply means "adding the opposite"). Simplify
to $5x = 8x - 16$. Subtract $8x$ from each side to get

$-3x = -16$, so $x = \frac{16}{3}$.

8

Example: *What is the value of x in $\dfrac{x + 12}{x + 4} = \dfrac{3}{2}$?*

Solution: Our first step would be $2(x + 12) = 3(x + 4)$, which becomes $2x + 24 = 3x + 12$. You know the ropes by now!

$2x + 24 - 24 = 3x + 12 - 2 -24$

$2x = 3x - 12$

$2x - 3x = 3x - 3x -12$

$-1x = -12$, so $x = 12$

Be sure you were not tempted to divide 4 into 12! You would have incorrectly written $\dfrac{x + 3}{x + 1} = \dfrac{3}{2}$, which would lead to a <u>wrong</u> answer of 3. Incidentally, by substitution, you can verify that 12 is the correct answer.

1. **Which one of the following ratios is <u>not</u> equal to the other three choices?**

   (A) $\dfrac{12}{40}$ (C) $\dfrac{20}{65}$

   (B) $\dfrac{15}{50}$ (D) $\dfrac{\frac{3}{5}}{2}$

   For 2–10, solve for *x*.

   2. $\dfrac{14}{x} = \dfrac{3}{5}$ Answer: _____

3. $\dfrac{4}{15} = \dfrac{10}{x}$　　　　　　Answer: _____

4. $\dfrac{x}{0.03} = \dfrac{2.4}{16}$　　　　　　Answer: _____

5. $\dfrac{0.72}{x} = \dfrac{1.8}{7}$　　　　　　Answer: _____

6. $\dfrac{\frac{4}{3}}{18} = \dfrac{x}{\frac{5}{2}}$　　　　　　Answer: _____

7. $\dfrac{x}{36} = \dfrac{\frac{1}{9}}{\frac{4}{3}}$　　　　　　Answer: _____

8. $\dfrac{\frac{1}{8}}{\frac{2}{3}} = \dfrac{\frac{9}{10}}{x}$　　　　　　Answer: _____

9. $\dfrac{x-9}{x-15} = \dfrac{5}{3}$　　　　　　Answer: _____

10. $\dfrac{x+13}{10} = \dfrac{x}{4}$　　　　　　Answer: _____

Percents

In this lesson, we will explore the solution to percent problems using proportions. We will use the material you learned in Lesson 8 on proportions. Percents appear almost everywhere in our daily lives. Here are a few examples: (a) tips given for service in a restaurant, (b) price discounts on clothing, (c) price increases on rent, (d) commissions for salespeople.

Your Goal: When you have completed this lesson, you should be able to calculate any missing quantity in a percent problem, by setting up a proportion.

LESSON 9

Percents

The basic proportion we will use is $\dfrac{A}{B} = \dfrac{R}{100}$.

The best way to read this is as follows: A is a part of B as R percent is a part of 100 percent. Another way to read this is: A is R percent of B. In the examples that follow, A may be either larger or smaller than B. You should associate "R" with the word "rate."

1

Example: *What number is 20% of 85?*

Solution: The missing number is A. Use 20 as the value of R and 85 as the value of B. The proportion becomes $\dfrac{A}{85} = \dfrac{20}{100}$. Now, using the technique you learned in Lesson 8, with A as the variable, we get $100A = (85)(20) = 1700$, so $A = 17$. Note that we are looking for a part of 85 that represents 20%.

Another way to view this problem is to recall that 20% means $\dfrac{20}{100}$, which reduces to $\dfrac{1}{5}$; so we seek a number that is $\dfrac{1}{5}$ of 85, which means 85 divided by 5.

2

Example: *0.32% of 150 is what number?*

Solution: Don't get confused with the phrasing of this question! Hopefully, you see that the same quantity A is missing in our proportion. We are looking for a part of 150 that represents 0.32%. Our proportion is $\dfrac{A}{150} = \dfrac{0.32}{100}$.
Then, we get $100A = (150)(0.32) = 48$, so $A = 0.48$.

Example: *24 is what percent of 92? (to the nearest tenth)*

3

Solution: First, we recognize that 24 is the value of A, while 92 is the value of B. Since R is unknown, the proportion is $\frac{24}{92} = \frac{R}{100}$. Then, $92R = 2400$, so $R = 26.1$.

Whenever a number requires rounding, for peace of mind (yours and ours!), we'll indicate the level of accuracy needed. The actual answer would have been 26.08695652. . ., so rounding would be needed.

Example: *75 is what percent of 60?*

4

Solution: Here, we again have the values of A and B, but notice that A is the larger amount. Using Example 3 as a guideline, since R is unknown, the correct proportion is $\frac{75}{60} = \frac{R}{100}$. Then $60R = 7500$, so $R = 125$. Notice that our answer is greater than 100%, because 75 is greater than 60.

Example: *0.9 is 15% of what number?*

5

Solution: The phrase "of what number" should reveal to you which of A, B, or R is unknown. Hopefully, you agree that B is the unknown quantity. This means that 0.9 is the value of A and 15 is the value of R. Thus, the proportion is $\frac{0.9}{B} = \frac{15}{100}$. Then $15B = (0.9)(100) = 90$. So, $B = 6$.

Example: *4.5 is 250% of what number?*

6

Solution: Similar to Example 5, the B value is unknown. Using 4.5 as the value of A, and 250 as the value of R, the proportion is $\frac{4.5}{B} = \frac{250}{100}$. Then $250B = 450$, so $B = 1.8$.

Note that the value of A is larger than the value of B. However, you should not be surprised; the percent given is over 100.

Example: *11.2% of what number is 0.036? (to the nearest hundredth)*

Solution: Try to recognize this example as similar to the previous two examples. It can be rewritten as "0.036 is 11.2% of what number?" Once again, the value of *B* is unknown. Using 0.036 as the value of *A* and 11.2 as the value of *R*, the proportion is $\frac{0.036}{B} = \frac{11.2}{100}$.

As usual, we cross-multiply to get $11.2B = 3.6$. So, $B = 0.32$. The actual answer for *B* would be $0.32\overline{142857}$, so rounding off is definitely desired.

Example: *25 is 30% larger than what number? (to the nearest hundredth)*

Solution: Be careful here! If you simply make the same substitutions as you did in Examples 5, 6, and 7, your proportion will be wrong. Note that "larger" has replaced the word "of." The phrase: "30% larger than" means the same as "130% of." Rewrite the original question as "25 is 130% of what number?" Now we can use the given numbers correctly in the proportion where 25 is the value of *A*, 130 is the value of *R*, and the value of *B* is unknown.

The proportion is $\frac{25}{B} = \frac{130}{100}$.

Then $130B = 2500$, so $B = 19.23$.

Example: *61.6 is 12% smaller than what number?*

Solution: Once again, do not substitute directly into our proportion. The trick is to subtract the given percent labeled as "smaller" from 100%. Rewriting Example 9 as "61.6 is 88% of what number?" leads to $\frac{61.6}{B} = \frac{88}{100}$.

Then $88B = 6160$, so $B = 70$.

Note that we can <u>never</u> have more than "100% smaller."

Example: *56 is what percent larger than 50?*

10

Solution: Since 56 – 50 = 6, the original question can be rewritten as "6 is what percent of 50?" Now, by direct substitution into the proportion, $\frac{6}{50} = \frac{R}{100}$.
Then 50R = 600, so R = 12.

Example: *22.2 is what percent smaller than 40?*

11

Solution: Following the concept of Example 10, we calculate 40 – 22.2 = 17.8. Our original question becomes "17.8 is what percent of 40?" We know that A = 17.8, B = 40, and R is unknown, so the proportion is $\frac{17.8}{40} = \frac{R}{100}$.
Then 40R = 1780, so R = 44.5.

Example: *27 is what percent larger than 8?*

12

Solution: This example is much like Example 10. We calculate 27 – 8 = 19. Then the question translates to "19 is what percent of 8?" Using either Example 3 or 4, we know that 19 is the value of A, and 8 is the value of B. The proportion is $\frac{19}{8} = \frac{R}{100}$.
Then 8R = 1900, so R = 237.5.

MathFlash!

To check the answer to Example 12, note that 16 would be 100% larger than 8, and 24 would be 200% larger than 8. Since 27 is larger than 24, then 27 must be more than 200% larger than 8. Essentially, "100% larger" than any number means "twice" that number; "200% larger" than any number means "three times" that number; and so forth.

Example: *What number is 33.6% larger than 18? (to the nearest hundredth)*

13

Solution: This example looks similar to Examples 1 and 2, but the word "larger" is used in place of the word "of." Hopefully, you are comfortable with translating "33.6% larger" to "133.6% of." Then, the question can be rewritten as "What number is 133.6% of 18?" Using 133.6 as the value of R and 18 as the value of B, the proportion is $\dfrac{A}{18} = \dfrac{133.6}{100}$.

Then $100A = 2404.8$, so $A = 24.05$.

Example: *What number is 75% smaller than 251.2?*

14

Solution: Change "75% smaller" to "25% of," so that we are looking for a number that is 25% of 251.2. Using 251.2 as the value of B and 25 as the value of R, the proportion is $\dfrac{A}{251.2} = \dfrac{25}{100}$.

Then, $100A = 6280$, so $A = 62.8$.

 Test Yourself!

For each question, write a correct proportion, then solve.

1.   96 is 28% of what number? (to the nearest hundredth)

   Proportion: _____=_____ Answer: _____

2.   0.24 is what percent of 0.5?

   Proportion: _____=_____ Answer: _____

3.   200.55 is 5% larger than what number?

   Proportion: _____=_____ Answer: _____

Test Yourself! (continued)

4.   **What number is 1.3% of 84? (to the nearest hundredth)**

Proportion: _____ = _____   Answer: _____

5.   **What number is 11.5% smaller than 60?**

Proportion: _____ = _____   Answer: _____

6.   **44 is 280% of what number? (to the nearest hundredth)**

Proportion: _____ = _____   Answer: _____

7.   **16.5 is what percent smaller than 21? (to the nearest hundredth)**

Proportion: _____ = _____   Answer: _____

8.   **29.4 is what percent higher than 9.8 ?**

Proportion: _____ = _____   Answer: _____

9.   **What number is 0.45% larger than 120?**

Proportion: _____ = _____   Answer: _____

10.   **364 is 60% smaller than what number?**

Proportion: _____ = _____   Answer: _____

Word Problem Applications for Percents

In this lesson, we will explore word problem application to percent problems that use proportions. This material will be heavily based on what you learned in Lesson 9. You should be thoroughly familiar with the proportion $\frac{A}{B} = \frac{R}{100}$. Remember to read this proportion as: "A is R percent of B."

Your Goal: When you have completed this lesson, you should be able to determine the value of an unknown quantity in word problems that deal with percent increase or percent decrease.

LESSON 10

Word Problem Applications for Percents

Example: 1

In Wanda's weekly paycheck, 23% of her gross amount is deducted for taxes. If the actual amount deducted is $220.80, what is the gross amount of her paycheck?

Solution: We need to identify with which letter of $\dfrac{A}{B} = \dfrac{R}{100}$ each of the given numbers is associated. Once we recognize that $220.80 represents 23% of the unknown amount, we can conclude that $220.80 is the A value and that 23 is the R value. Since the B value is unknown, the proportion is $\dfrac{\$220.80}{B} = \dfrac{23}{100}$. By cross-multiplying, $23B = \$22{,}080$, so $B = \$960$.

Example: 2

Sally is shopping for a new pair of shoes, which normally costs $135. The shoe store is having a 15% sale on the shoes. How much will Sally pay?

Solution: First, we realize that Sally will pay 100% − 15% = 85% of the normal cost of the shoes. This means we are seeking a number that is 85% of $135. Although there is a quick way to complete this example arithmetically, let's use the proportional method. The value of R is 85 and the value of B is $135. The proportion becomes $\dfrac{A}{\$135} = \dfrac{85}{100}$. Then $100A = \$11{,}475$, so $A = \$114.75$.

Example: *Bobby wants to buy a used car from the Trust-Us Car Company. The car Bobby wants costs $880; however, he only has $200 to pay as a down payment.*
What percent down payment is he paying? (to the nearest tenth)

Solution: This is a very direct application of the proportion $\frac{A}{B} = \frac{R}{100}$. The value of A is $200, and the value of B is $880. The proportion will read as $\frac{\$200}{\$880} = \frac{R}{100}$. Then $880R = 20{,}000$, so $R = 22.73$, which means 22.73%.

Example: *Kelli sold 90 insurance policies this month. This number represents a 125% increase over her sales last month.*
How many insurance policies did Kelli sell last month?

Solution: Recall that an increase of 125% means that the new number is actually 225% of the original number. Thus, 90 represents 225% of an unknown number, because the original number is 100% of itself. In our famous proportion, that unknown number is represented by B. We write $\frac{90}{B} = \frac{225}{100}$, from which we get $225B = 9000$. So, $B = 40$.

Example: *The enrollment at Small Campus University dropped from 5600 last year to 5012 this year.*
What percent decrease does this represent?

Solution: The percent decrease corresponds to the actual number drop in enrollment from last year to this year. We note that $5600 - 5012 = 588$, and this is the number that corresponds to the percent decrease. Also, remember that the percent decrease is based on the <u>higher</u> enrollment number, which is 5600. This means that 588 is an unknown percent of 5600. The proportion will be $\frac{588}{5600} = \frac{R}{100}$. Then $5600R = 58{,}800$, so $R = 10.5$.
The university had a 10.5% decrease in enrollment.

Example: *The Hard Luck Machine Company has fallen on hard times. From the year 2000 to the present, the staff size has dropped by 64%. There are currently only 270 staff members. What was the staff size in the year 2000?*

Solution: The current staff of 270 must represent $100\% - 64\% = 36\%$ of the staff size in the year 2000. Translated, we are asking "270 is 36% of what number?" The missing quantity in our proportion is B, so that $\dfrac{270}{B} = \dfrac{36}{100}$. Then $36B = 27{,}000$, so $B = 750$.

Example: *Jaclyn is a student in Mr. Harmon's class. She has accumulated a total of 500 points on her exams. Mr. Harmon told her that if she can increase her point total by 7.2%, she will earn a grade of A for the course.*
How many additional points does Jaclyn need to earn an A grade?

Solution: The number of additional points needed is 7.2% of 500, so in our proportion, the value of R is 7.2, and the value of B is 500. Of course, the A value is unknown, so we write $\dfrac{A}{500} = \dfrac{7.2}{100}$. Then $100A = 3600$, so $A = 36$ points.

Example: *Kenny is also a student in Mr. Harmon's class. He has accumulated a total of 480 points on his exams. Mr. Harmon told him that if he can increase his point total by at least 2.5%, he will earn a grade of B for the course.*
What is the minimum number of total points Kenny needs to earn a grade of B?

Solution: Since we are looking for a number that is 2.5% larger than 480, this number is 102.5% of 480. In our proportion, the value of A is unknown, the value of B is 480, and the value of R is 102.5. Then, $\dfrac{A}{480} = \dfrac{102.5}{100}$, followed by $100A = 49{,}200$. So $A = 492$.

Hopefully, you are <u>not</u> confusing this value of A with the grade of A. In truth, remember that the letter A used in the proportion is just an ordinary variable. Any other letter could have been used for the unknown in Examples 7 and 8, and we would have gotten the same answers.

Example: *In basketball, Laura's average number of points per game is 160% of Jane's average number of points per game. Laura's average number of points is 40.*
What is Jane's average number of points?

9

Solution: The correct interpretation is the question: "40 is 160% of what number?" Thus, the value of A is 40, and the value of R is 160. The proportion is $\dfrac{40}{B} = \dfrac{160}{100}$. Then $160B = 4000$, so $B = 25$.

Example: *Jim's annual salary rose from $38,000 to $45,000.*
What percent increase does this represent? (to the nearest tenth)

10

Solution: We first calculate $45,000 – $38,000 = $7000, which is the increase in salary. The question then becomes: "$7000 is what percent of $38,000?" Using $7000 as the value of A and $38,000 as the value of B, the proportion is $\dfrac{7000}{38,000} = \dfrac{R}{100}$. Then $38,000R = 700,000$, so $R = 18.4$. This means that Jim's salary rose by 18.4%.

Test Yourself!

Write an appropriate proportion and solve.

1. The population of a small town increased by 5.5% since last year. If this year's population is 422, what was the population last year?

    Proportion: _____ = _____ *Answer:* _____

2. Chelsea just bought a GPS navigation system for her car. The GPS normally sells for $360. However, this item was on sale, so it was discounted by 22%. How much did Chelsea pay for this system?

    Proportion: _____ = _____ *Answer:* _____

3. A chemist is mixing a solution that is a combination of a newly developed acid and water. The entire solution is 600 milliliters, of which 98 milliliters is water.
    What percent of this solution is water? (to the nearest tenth)

    Proportion: _____ = _____ *Answer:* _____

4. A rare coin is expected to increase in value by 16.25% next year. This year, the coin is worth $1100. What will be its value next year?

    Proportion: _____ = _____ *Answer:* _____

5. Yolanda's cat used to weigh 18.6 pounds. After a one-year diet, the cat now weighs 13.2 pounds. To the nearest whole number, what percent weight loss did Yolanda's cat experience?

    Proportion: _____ = _____ *Answer:* _____

6. Sam sells sailboats for the Harbor Company. Last week, he earned a commission of $352 on a particular sailboat. If his commission rate is 11%, what was the selling price of this sailboat?

    Proportion: _____ = _____ *Answer:* _____

7. A flu epidemic has just spread through the village of Parkville. In a 24-hour period, the number of patients admitted to the local clinic as a result of this epidemic rose from 35 to 112.
What percent increase does this represent in this 24-hour period?

    Proportion: _____ = _____ 　*Answer:* _____

8. At a large college, there were 12,000 students enrolled at the beginning of the current semester. Due to students withdrawing or transferring to other colleges, the enrollment dropped by 24.7% by the end of the semester.
How many students were enrolled at the end of the semester?

    Proportion: _____ = _____ 　*Answer:* _____

9. Mike is shooting foul shots in basketball. Out of 128 tries, he makes 80 shots.
What percent of his shots did he miss?

    Proportion: _____ = _____ 　*Answer:* _____

10. Sharon just received a weekly salary increase of $324. This represents an 18% increase over her previous weekly salary.
What was her former salary?

    Proportion: _____ = _____ 　*Answer:* _____

LESSONS 6-10

QUIZ TWO

1. Roland's dog currently weighs 15 pounds. Last year, his dog weighed 13.5 pounds. To the nearest whole number, what percent weight gain did Roland's dog experience?

   A 10%

   B 11%

   C 12%

   D 13%

2. What is the value of x in the equation $\dfrac{x}{0.48} = \dfrac{6}{0.8}$?

   A 0.036

   B 0.36

   C 3.6

   D 36

3. Stacy has just started a new job in which she is paid an hourly wage for every hour up through 30 hours. For each hour after 30 hours, she gets an hourly bonus of 60%. This week, her gross pay is $475.20 for a total of 36 hours. What is her regular hourly wage for the first 30 hours?

   A $12.00

   B $13.20

   C $14.00

   D $15.80

4. What is the value of x in the equation $\dfrac{15}{x} = \dfrac{11}{x-3}$?

   A $\dfrac{15}{26}$

   B $\dfrac{45}{26}$

   C $\dfrac{15}{4}$

   D $\dfrac{45}{4}$

5. At a publishing company, each employee just received a holiday bonus of 15% of his or her regular weekly pay. Carlos calculated his bonus to be $87. What was his weekly pay, including the holiday bonus?

   A $580

   B $587

   C $667

   D $690

6. Pauline is a collector of rare silver and gold coins. Each silver coin costs $7, and each gold coin costs $12. She has decided to buy 24 silver coins. If she does not wish to spend more than $450 for all the coins, what is the maximum number of gold coins that she can buy?

   A   22

   B   23

   C   24

   D   25

7. What number is 32.5% smaller than 50?

   A   37.88

   B   33.75

   C   17.5

   D   16.25

8. Bret would like to buy a new television, which is selling for $420. He can afford to make a down payment of 18%. There are no additional charges. How much money will he owe after making this down payment?

   A $73.60

   B $233.00

   C $344.40

   D $402.00

9. The Neutron Toy Company is developing a new game. The company will have fixed costs totaling $150,000 plus $24 for each game that it sells. Each game will sell for $45. What is the minimum number of games that the company must sell in order to make a profit?

   A   7134

   B   7137

   C   7140

   D   7143

10. The number 1400 is what percent larger than 1380? (to the nearest hundredth of one percent)

   A   1.45%

   B   1.43%

   C   0.14%

   D   0.04%

Direct Variation

In this lesson, we will explore direct variation, which is sometimes called direct proportion. This variation requires two variables instead of one variable. Although any letters may be used to represent the two variables, we will use the familiar *x* and *y* letters. In the introduction to Lesson 8, we had mentioned that comparing map distance versus actual distance is an application of proportions. In particular, the length of the distance on the map between two cities varies directly with the actual distance between those cities.

Referring to the illustration of Lesson 8, notice that 4 inches is four times 1 inch; similarly, 200 miles is four times 50 miles. Using this map, suppose the two given cities were actually 600 miles apart. Since 600 miles is 12 times 50 miles, the map distance would be 12 times 1 inch, which is 12 inches.

Your Goal: When you have completed this lesson, you will be able to identify examples of direct variation as well as solve word problems that use this variation.

LESSON 11

Direct Variation

Definition: y varies directly as x if both variables either increase or decrease proportionally. This means that if the x value doubles, then the y value must also double. Similarly, if the x value is reduced to one-third of its value, the y value must also be reduced to one-third of its value. If y varies directly as x, then it is also true that x varies directly as y.

We will use x_1 (say "x sub one") to represent the first x value and x_2 to represent the second x value.

Likewise, let y_1 and y_2 represent the first and second y values.

The proportion we can use to show direct variation is $\dfrac{x_1}{x_2} = \dfrac{y_1}{y_2}$.

Example: *The cost for cleaning a carpet varies directly as the carpet's area.*
1 *Suppose that the cost for cleaning an area of 30 square feet is $75. What is the cost for cleaning an area of 50 square feet?*

Solution: Let the x's represent the areas, and let the y's represent the cost. We know each of the areas, but we don't know the second cost (y_2). Then, dropping the units of square feet and dollars, we can write $\dfrac{30}{50} = \dfrac{75}{y_2}$. Cross-multiplying, $30y_2 = 3750$. So, $y_2 = \$125$.

Example: *The number of pages in a novel that Luann can read varies*
2 *directly with time. If she can read 6 pages in 21 minutes, how many pages can she read in 49 minutes?*

Solution: Let the x's represent the number of pages read, and let the y's represent the time in minutes. The proportion is $\dfrac{6}{x_2} = \dfrac{21}{49}$. Then $21x_2 = 294$, so $x_2 = 14$ pages.
In this example, we were given both y values, but we didn't know x_2.

Example: *The number of miles a car can travel varies directly as the number of gallons of gas that it uses. When the car travels 35 miles, it uses 1.8 gallons of gas. How many miles could this car travel using 3.2 gallons of gas?*

3

Solution: Let the x's represent the gallons of gas and let the y's represent the number of miles traveled. Then we can write $\frac{1.8}{3.2} = \frac{35}{y_2}$.

Then, $1.8y_2 = (3.2)(35) = 112$. So, $y_2 = 62.22$ miles. (The actual answer is $62.\overline{2}$, but we rounded it off to the nearest hundredth.)

MathFlash!

Usually, we can round off answers to the nearest hundredth, but be aware of the units in each problem. In some cases, only a whole number should be used as the final answer.

The next three examples will illustrate this concept.

Example: *Suzanne is hosting a huge party. From previous experience, she knows that 200 pounds of potato salad can feed 300 people. If Suzanne orders 125 pounds of potato salad, how many people will that amount feed, if each person gets an equal portion?*

4

Solution: Let the x's represent the number of people, and let the y's represent the number of pounds of potato salad.

Then, since x_2 is unknown, we can write $\frac{300}{x_2} = \frac{200}{125}$. This means $200x_2 = 37,500$. Solving, $x_2 = 187.5$. (In this case, we must round <u>down</u>, so the answer is 187 people. We cannot have 0.5 of a person!)

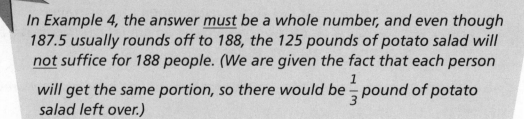

MathFlash!

In Example 4, the answer <u>must</u> be a whole number, and even though 187.5 usually rounds off to 188, the 125 pounds of potato salad will <u>not</u> suffice for 188 people. (We are given the fact that each person will get the same portion, so there would be $\frac{1}{3}$ pound of potato salad left over.)

Example: *For a certain construction project, it is estimated that if 22 people are hired, the project will cost $2300. Assuming that the number of people varies directly as the cost of the project, approximately how many people should be hired if only $1950 is allocated for this project?*

5

Solution: Let the *x*'s represent the cost, and let the *y*'s represent the number of people. We do not know y_2, so we have $\frac{2300}{1950} = \frac{22}{y_2}$. Then, $2300y_2 = 42{,}900$. So $y_2 = 18.65$ (rounded off).

Since the question asked for <u>approximately</u> how many people should be hired, the correct answer is 19. In this example, you should round off your answer to the nearest integer.

Example: *In the town of Spartanville, a home that is worth $270,000 is assessed an annual property tax of $5400. Assuming that the price of a home varies directly as its property tax, what is the property tax, to the nearest dollar, for a home that is worth $310,000?*

6

Solution: Let the *x*'s represent the value of the houses, and let the *y*'s represent the property taxes. We do not know y_2, so we have $\frac{270{,}000}{310{,}000} = \frac{5400}{y_2}$. Then $270{,}000y_2 = 1{,}674{,}000{,}000$. So, $y_2 = \$6200$.

Example: *Jeanette is baking her favorite cake. The directions state that she should use $\frac{3}{4}$ teaspoon of vanilla syrup for each $\frac{4}{5}$ cup of milk. If the cake requires $2\frac{1}{2}$ teaspoons of vanilla syrup, how much milk is required? (Assume that the amount of vanilla syrup varies directly with the amount of milk.)*

7

Solution: Let the x's represent the number of cups of milk, and let the y's represent the number of teaspoons of vanilla syrup. We don't know x_2, so we use $\frac{\frac{4}{5}}{x_2} = \frac{\frac{3}{4}}{2\frac{1}{2}}$. The next step is $\frac{3}{4}x_2 = \frac{4}{5} \times \frac{5}{2} = 2$. Then $x_2 = 2 \times \frac{4}{3} = \frac{8}{3}$ cups of milk.

Let's Review
SEE LESSON **8**

Note that this answer is not rounded off, since there was no direction to do so. Also, cups of milk can certainly be expressed in fractional form.

8

Example: *For a certain type of floor cleaner it is recommended that $\frac{2}{3}$ cup of the cleaner be used with $1\frac{1}{4}$ gallons of water. If cleaning all the floors of an office requires 6 gallons of water, how many cups of cleaner are needed?*

Solution: Let the x's represent the number of gallons of water, and let the y's represent the number of cups of cleaner. We are missing y_2, so our proportion is $\frac{1\frac{1}{4}}{6} = \frac{\frac{2}{3}}{x_2}$. We cross-multiply to get $1\frac{1}{4}x_2 = 6 \times \frac{2}{3} = 4$. Finally, $x_2 = 4 \div 1\frac{1}{4} = \frac{4}{1} \times \frac{4}{5} = \frac{16}{5}$ cups of cleaner.

Test Yourself!

For each question, write an appropriate proportion and solve.

1.   The actual height of a person varies directly as the person's height in a photograph. In real life, Lance is 70 inches tall. In a recent photo of him and his wife, Julie, Lance's height is 8 inches, and Julie's height is 7 inches. What is Julie's actual height in inches? (Do not round off.)

      Proportion: _____ = _____   *Answer:* _____

2.   Tonya is mowing her lawn. The time required to mow a specific area of grass varies directly with the area. If she can mow 32 square feet in 5 minutes, and she requires 123 minutes to mow the entire lawn, approximately how many square feet, as a whole number, is her entire lawn?

      Proportion: _____ = _____   *Answer:* _____

3.   Jennifer is a key administrative assistant in the Great Results Company. One of the items that she is ordering for a company banquet is macaroni salad. From previous experience, she knows that 20 pounds of macaroni salad will serve 8 people. If Jennifer orders 225 pounds of macaroni salad, how many people can be fed, assuming that each person gets an equal portion?

      Proportion: _____ = _____   *Answer:* _____

4.   Joanne and Larry Williams own a small business. Last year, their income was $430,000, and they had to pay $19,350 in state taxes. Assuming that income varies directly with state taxes, how much money in state taxes will they owe if their income this year is $510,000?

      Proportion: _____ = _____   *Answer:* _____

Test Yourself! *(continued)*

5. There is a bridge in Pleasant Pines, Maine, that is 400 yards long and can support a maximum of 65 cars at the same time. If a similar bridge that is 330 yards long is being built in St. Louis, what is the maximum number of cars it can support at the same time? You can assume that the length of the bridge varies directly as the number of cars on it.

    Proportion: _____ =_____   *Answer:* _____

6. The distance between Seattle and San Francisco is represented by 25 inches on a huge wall map. The actual distance between them is 680 miles. If the distance between El Paso and Dallas is 1025 miles, to the nearest hundredth, how many inches apart are they on this wall map?

    Proportion: _____ =_____   *Answer:* _____

7. Wally can process 16 invoice orders in 44 minutes. Assuming that the number of invoice orders that he can process varies directly as time, how many minutes would be required for him to process 36 invoice orders?

    Proportion: _____ =_____   *Answer:* _____

8. In the town of Island Village, a house that is worth $344,000 is assessed an annual property tax of $5160. Marcella, a resident of Island Village, just received her annual property tax bill for $9288. Assuming that the value of a house varies directly as its annual property tax, what is the value of her house?

    Proportion: _____ =_____   *Answer:* _____

9.   If 10 U.S. dollars are worth the same as 13 Canadian dollars, approximately how many U.S. dollars are the same as 100 Canadian dollars?

Proportion: _____ = _____   Answer: _____

10.   Roger is baking his favorite muffins. The directions state that $\frac{1}{6}$ cup of milk should be used for each $1\frac{1}{2}$ spoonfuls of vegetable oil. If he decides to use $\frac{3}{8}$ cup of milk, how many spoonfuls of vegetable oil are needed? You can assume that the amount of milk varies directly as the amount of vegetable oil.

Proportion: _____ = _____   Answer: _____

Inverse Variation

In this lesson, we will explore inverse variation, which is sometimes called inverse proportion. Similar to direct variation, which was addressed in Lesson 11, this type of variation requires two variables instead of one variable. Although any letters may be used to represent the two variables, we'll still use the familiar *x* and *y* letters. One real-life application of inverse variation involves rate and time when traveling a specific distance: the faster you travel, the less time you need and the slower you move, the more time you need. Often when things change, they change in the same direction. For instance, if you work more hours, you get paid more.

Your Goal: When you have completed this lesson, you will be able to identify examples of inverse variation as well as solve word problems that use this variation.

LESSON 12

Inverse Variation

Definition: *y* varies inversely as *x* if when one variable increases, the other variable decreases proportionally.

This means that if the *x* value is doubled, then the y value must be divided by 2. (It is also true that *x* varies inversely as *y*.) Let x_1 represent the first *x* value, and x_2 represent the second *x* value.
Let y_1 and y_2 represent the first and second *y* values.

Then the proportion we can use to show inverse variation is $\dfrac{x_1}{x_2} = \dfrac{y_2}{y_1}$.

Use extra care when applying this proportion. The first *y* value belongs on the **bottom** of the right-hand fraction. As in direct variation problems, it is not important which quantity is assigned to the *x*'s and which quantity is assigned to the *y*'s. However, you must be consistent within the problem.

Example:

1

In going from City A to City B, a car traveling at an average speed of 45 miles per hour can cover this distance in 33 minutes.
If speed varies inversely as time, how many minutes would this trip take if the car were traveling at 40 miles per hour? (to the nearest tenth)

Solution:

Let the *x*'s represent speed in miles per hour, and let the *y*'s represent the time in minutes. We know each of the speeds, but we don't know the second time (y_2). Then, dropping the units of miles per hour and minutes, we can write $\dfrac{45}{40} = \dfrac{y_2}{33}$. (Remember that the first *y* value belongs on the <u>bottom</u> of the right-hand fraction.)
Cross-multiplying, we get $40y_2 = (45)(33) = 1485$.
Then $y_2 = 37.1$ minutes.

Example: *In order to have a large picnic, each person has agreed to pay the same amount of money. If 60 people attend, each person will pay $15. The number of people attending varies inversely as the cost per person.*
What will be the cost per person if only 50 people attend?

2

Solution: Let the x's represent the number of people, and let the y's represent the cost in dollars.

The proportion is $\frac{60}{50} = \frac{y_2}{15}$. Then $50y_2 = 900$, so $y_2 = \$18$.

Example: *At Learning Tree University, the tuition charged per student varies inversely as the number of students. This year, the student enrollment is 5200 and the tuition is $800 per student. The university forecasts that the student enrollment for next year will be 5500.*
To the nearest dollar, what should be the tuition per student next year?

3

Solution: Let the x's represent the student enrollment, and let the y's

represent the tuition per student. The proportion is $\frac{5200}{5500} = \frac{y_2}{800}$.

Then $5500y_2 = 4{,}160{,}000$, so $y_2 = \$756$ (approximately).

Example: *Here is a situation that is applicable to the field of physics. If the temperature is kept constant, the pressure of a gas inside a closed container varies inversely as the volume of gas in that container. Suppose that the pressure of nitrogen is 16 pounds per square inch inside a large container in which the volume of nitrogen is 5.5 cubic inches.*
If the volume of the nitrogen is expanded to 6.4 cubic inches, what is the corresponding pressure in pounds per square inch?

4

Solution: Let the x's represent the volume in cubic inches, and let the y's represent the pressure in pounds per square inch. As usual, you need not worry about the units that are used. The proportion is

$\frac{5.5}{6.4} = \frac{y_2}{16}$. Then $6.4y_2 = 88$, so $y_2 = 13.75$ pounds per square inch.

Example:

> *At a local swim club, the owner has noticed that the number of people who use the pool during any one month varies inversely as the number of rainy days during that month. During last July, which had 20 rainy days, a total of 1050 people used the pool. The forecast for next July predicts only 8 rainy days.*
>
> *What is the owner's best estimate for the number of people who will use the pool next July?*

5

Solution:

Let the x's represent the number of rainy days, and let the y's represent the number of people who use the pool. The proportion is $\dfrac{20}{8} = \dfrac{y_2}{1050}$. Then $8y_2 = 21{,}000$, so $y_2 = 2625$ people.

Example:

> *Here is a different way of doing a geometry problem involving a triangle. For any triangle in which the area is constant, the base varies inversely as the height. You are given a triangle in which the base is 8.5 inches and the height is 7.2 inches.*
>
> *Assuming that the area remains constant, what is the base of this triangle in which its height is changed to 15 inches?*

6

Solution:

Let the x's represent the heights, and let the y's represent the bases. The proportion is $\dfrac{7.2}{15} = \dfrac{y_2}{8.5}$. Then $15y_2 = 61.2$, so $y_2 = 4.08$ inches. Remember, you should not round off unless the directions say so. An answer of 4.1 would have been acceptable if the directions stated that the answer should be rounded off to the nearest tenth.

1. In any inverse proportion involving *x* and *y*, when the value of *x* is multiplied by 4, what change takes place for *y*?

(A)   It gets multiplied by 4.   (C)   It gets increased by 4.

(B)   It gets divided by 4.   (D)   It gets decreased by 4.

For 2–10, write an appropriate proportion and solve.

2. Joe has a certain amount of money in his pocket. If the price of gasoline is $2.75 per gallon, he can buy 8 gallons of gas for his car. Suppose the price of gasoline rises to $2.95 per gallon.
To the nearest hundredth, how many gallons of gas can he buy?

Proportion: _____ = _____   Answer: _____

3. For any rectangle in which the area is constant, the length varies inversely as the width. Suppose a rectangle has a length of 20 cm and a width of 5.6 cm.
If the width is changed to 8.96 cm, what will be the new length?

Proportion: _____ = _____   Answer: _____

4. In traveling from Philadelphia to Raleigh, a train that averages 75 miles per hour can cover this distance in 280 minutes.
Since speed varies inversely as time, how many average miles per hour would be necessary if the train were to cover this distance in just 230 minutes? (to the nearest tenth)

Proportion: _____ = _____   Answer: _____

5.   Mrs. Johnson's class is taking a bus to Orlando. Each of the 30 children in her class has agreed to pay $12.50 for the bus trip. Unfortunately, 5 of the children decided they do not want to go on this trip.
How much extra money will each of the remaining 25 children have to pay? Assume that the total cost remains the same.

Proportion: _____=_____   *Answer:* _____

6.   To complete a very large project at the Uniform Testing Company, 12 people would each be required to spend 18 hours working on it. However, the management team has decided that the limit of time for each person to work on the project should be only 8 hours. The number of people needed varies inversely with the individual number of hours worked.
How many people will be needed for this project?

Proportion: _____=_____   *Answer:* _____

7.   With a constant temperature, the pressure of a gas inside a closed container varies inversely as the volume of gas in that container. In a large container, suppose that the pressure of propane is 21.5 pounds per square inch and its volume is 10 cubic inches.
If the pressure is increased to 25 pounds per square inch, what will be the corresponding volume of the propane?

Proportion: _____=_____   *Answer:* _____

8.   At High Tech High School, the cost per student for a school lunch varies inversely with the number of students enrolled. The current enrollment is 1960, and the current cost of a school lunch is $3.40. Next year, the projected enrollment is only 1850. What should be the cost of a school lunch next year? (to the nearest cent)

Proportion: _____=_____   *Answer:* _____

Test Yourself! (continued)

9.   In an electrical circuit, the current is inversely proportional to the resistance. Suppose the current is 120 amperes when the resistance is 45 ohms.
     In this circuit, what is the current when the resistance is 60 ohms?

     Proportion: _____ = _____   *Answer:* _____

10. At a local newspaper, the circulation manager has noticed that the number of subscribers varies inversely with the cost of a year's subscription. This year, there are 6400 subscribers, each of whom pays $36 for a one-year subscription. The company would like to have 8000 subscribers next year.
     What will the newspaper have to charge for a subscription next year?

     Proportion: _____ = _____   *Answer:* _____

Exponents, Multiplication, and Division—Part 1

In this lesson, we will explore the rules of exponents. We will use these rules to perform multiplication and division in algebraic expressions. As a quick review, recall that 5^3 means $(5)(5)(5) = 125$. Likewise, $\left(-\frac{1}{3}\right)^2$ means $\left(-\frac{1}{3}\right)\left(-\frac{1}{3}\right) = \frac{1}{9}$.

Your Goal: When you have completed this lesson, you will be able to use the basic rules of exponents to both multiply and divide several types of algebraic expressions.

Exponents, Multiplication, and Division—Part 1

1 **Example:** *What is an equivalent expression for $(4^2)(4^3)$?*

Solution: One way to find this product is to simplify each quantity in parentheses first, so that it reads (16)(64), which is 1024. If you are curious about how this answer can be written as a power of 4, there is an easy way to do that. Note that if you calculated 4^5, which means (4)(4)(4)(4)(4), you get 1024.

Based on this example, a shortcut would have been to keep the same base 4 and use the sum of the exponents as the correct power in the answer. The answer is 4^5.

2 **Example:** *What is an equivalent expression for $(-3)^1(-3)^3$?*

Solution: Simplifying each quantity in parentheses first, we have $(-3)(-27) = 81$. Note that $(-3)^4$ has the value of 81, so again it appears that all we had to do was use the same base of -3 and add the exponents 1 and 3. The answer is $(-3)^4$.

3 **Example:** *What is an equivalent expression for $(6^4)(6^7)$?*

Solution: If you are anticipating that the answer can be written as 6^{11}, you are right on target! Here is an explanation as to why adding exponents and retaining the base number always works. 6^4 means (6)(6)(6)(6), and 6^7 means (6)(6)(6)(6)(6)(6)(6).

By substitution, you can see that this entire problem is really a product of eleven 6's. It actually looks like the following: [(6)(6)(6)(6)][(6)(6)(6)(6)(6)(6)(6)].

4

Example: *How would you simplify $(x^3)(x^4)$?*

Solution: The product will be found by retaining x and simply adding the exponents. The answer is x^7. View this as a group of three x's multiplied by a group of four x's, and this leads to a group of seven x's, which means x^7.

5

Example: *How would you simplify $(z^8)(z)$?*

Solution: First, let's recognize that just as a number such as 12 means 12^1, the same is true of any variable (letter). This means that $z = z^1$. Using the same technique as in the previous examples, $(z^8)(z) = z^9$.

RULE 1   When multiplying expressions with the same base, **use the base as part of the answer and add the corresponding exponents**. Caution: Do not actually multiply the bases. For example, $(2^4)(2^2) = 2^6$, <u>not</u> 4^6.

6

Example: *What is an equivalent expression for $\dfrac{5^5}{5^3}$?*

Solution: If you had no exponent rules to guide you, your only course of action would be to calculate 5^5 as 3125 and calculate 5^3 as 125; then divide 3125 by 125 to get the answer of 25. You already know that $25 = 5^2$. Hopefully, you observe that using the base of 5, we could have found the answer of 5^2 by simply subtracting the exponent 3 from the exponent 5.

The reason that this works is because you can rewrite the initial problem, without exponents, as $\dfrac{(5)(5)(5)(5)(5)}{(5)(5)(5)}$. Each 5 in the denominator can be cancelled with one of the 5's in the numerator. After all the 5's in the denominator are cancelled, there would be two 5's remaining in the numerator. $\dfrac{(\cancel{5})(\cancel{5})(\cancel{5})(5)(5)}{(\cancel{5})(\cancel{5})(\cancel{5})}$. This leads to the answer of 5^2 (which is 25).

Example: *What is an equivalent expression for $\dfrac{(-8)^7}{(-8)^4}$?*

7

Solution: If you were to write out this example without exponents, you would see the following: $\dfrac{(-8)(-8)(-8)(-8)(-8)(-8)(-8)}{(-8)(-8)(-8)(-8)}$.

Similar to Example 6, we can cancel a pair of –8s, one from the numerator and one from the denominator, four times. $\dfrac{(\cancel{-8})(\cancel{-8})(\cancel{-8})(\cancel{-8})(-8)(-8)(-8)}{(\cancel{-8})(\cancel{-8})(\cancel{-8})(\cancel{-8})}$. This would leave only three –8's in the numerator, so the answer is $(-8)^3$.

MathFlash!

Be sure that you do <u>not</u> divide the bases. Only subtract the exponents.

Example: *How do you simplify $\dfrac{y^6}{y^3}$?*

8

Solution: Let's approach this example in the same fashion as in Examples 6 and 7. We can rewrite this as $\dfrac{(y)(y)(y)(y)(y)(y)}{(y)(y)(y)}$. Now, you can cancel three y's from the numerator and three y's from the denominator, so that you are left with three y's in the numerator. The answer is y^3. As you look over the results from Examples 6, 7, and 8, it appears that all we needed to do was retain the given base and perform a subtraction with the exponents.

MathFlash!

Do <u>not</u> fall into the trap of dividing exponents! This is a mistake that can easily happen. Try to visualize the cancellation of a common number of bases. In this way, when you see an example such as $\dfrac{x^{20}}{x^5}$, you realize that when the five x's in the denominator are cancelled with five of the x's in the numerator, there are still fifteen x's left in the numerator. Thus, the answer must be x^{15}, and <u>not</u> x^4.

RULE 2   When dividing expressions with the same base, **use the base** as part of the answer and **subtract the exponent** used in the denominator from the exponent used in the numerator. Caution: Do not actually divide the bases. For example, $\dfrac{9^4}{9} = \dfrac{9^4}{9^1} = 9^3$, not 1^3. Likewise, $\dfrac{x^7}{x^2} = x^5$, not 1^5.

9   **Example:**   *What is an equivalent expression for $(x^3)^4$?*

Solution: If you are thinking that the answer is x^7, you jumped to a common (but mistaken) conclusion. In truth, x^7 would be correct if the example had read $(x^3)(x^4)$. To find the correct answer, we must recognize that $(x^3)^4$ means $(x^3)(x^3)(x^3)(x^3)$. Each one of these parentheses contains three x's that are multiplied. Since there are four sets of parentheses, each of which contains a product of three x's, we are actually multiplying x by itself 12 times! Our answer must be x^{12}.

Note that the correct exponent is just the product of the two original exponents in the example. It is also the sum of the exponents of $(x^3)(x^3)(x^3)(x^3)$.

10   **Example:**   *What is an equivalent expression for $(5^6)^3$?*

Solution: Remember that this is not the same as $(5^6)(5^3)$. You could rewrite the example as $(5^6)(5^6)(5^6)$. Each of these parentheses contains six 5's that are multiplied. Then, how many 5's are being multiplied when counting all three parentheses? You will see that there are eighteen 5's, so our answer should be 5^{18}.

Note again that the exponent 18 is simply the product of the original exponents in the example. It is also the sum of the three 6's in $(5^6)(5^6)(5^6)$. Note that you need to use your calculator to check your answer: $5^6 = 15{,}625$ and $(15{,}625)^3 \approx 3.815 \times 10^{12}$, which is the value of 5^{18}.

RULE 3   When given a number written as a base and exponent that is also being raised to an exponent, simply **multiply the two exponents**. The base remains as is.

1. Which one of the following is equivalent to $(7^5)(7^3)$?

    (A) 7^2 (C) 7^{15}

    (B) 7^8 (D) 49^8

2. Which one of the following is equivalent to $\dfrac{9^{10}}{9^2}$?

    (A) 3^8 (C) 9^8

    (B) 9^5 (D) 9^{12}

3. Which one of the following is equivalent to 36^{20}?

    (A) $(36^2)^{10}$ (C) $(6^{14})(6^6)$

    (B) $(36^{10})^{10}$ (D) $(6^{18})^2$

For 4–10, write each expression in its simplest form.

4. $(x^{12})(x^3)$ Answer: _____

5. $\dfrac{y^{22}}{y^2}$ Answer: _____

6. $(w^7)^5$ Answer: _____

7. $(z^{16})(z)$ Answer: _____

8. $\dfrac{x^{27}}{x^3}$ Answer: _____

9. $(y^{11})(y^{12})$ Answer: _____

10. $(z^4)^{10}$ Answer: _____

Exponents, Multiplication, and Division—Part 2

In this lesson, we will explore the rules of exponents, with respect to multiplication and in more involved algebraic expressions. At this point, you may want to review the five properties of numbers that were discussed in Lesson 5, especially the Distributive Property of Multiplication Over Addition.

Your Goal: When you have completed this lesson, you will be able to multiply some algebraic expressions.

LESSON 14

Exponents, Multiplication, and Division—Part 2

1

Example: *What expression is equivalent to (3)(x + 5) without parentheses?*

Solution: In this example, 3 is being multiplied by the quantity $x + 5$. Recalling the Distributive Property of Multiplication Over Addition (and Subtraction), we will multiply 3 by x, then 3 by 5. The product of 3 and x is commonly written as $3x$, and the product of 3 and 5 is 15. The answer is $3x + 15$.

MathFlash!

Since 3x can have virtually any value, we cannot combine 3x with 15 to create one term. These are called unlike terms, so they can never be combined. Also, x3 is not written for the product of 3 and x, because it appears too similar to x^3.

2

Example: *What expression is equivalent to (–6)(x – 8) without parentheses?*

Solution: This example is quite similar to Example 1. First, multiply –6 by x, then multiply –6 by –8. The answer is $-6x + 48$.
Be careful that you don't write –48 in the answer because the product of 2 negative numbers is a positive number!

3

Example: *What expression is equivalent to (4w)(3w + 13) without parentheses?*

Solution: First multiply $4w$ by $3w$ to get $12w^2$, then multiply $4w$ by 13 to get $52w$. The answer is $12w^2 + 52w$.

MathFlash!

When you are multiplying single expressions such as 4w and 3w, you are technically using an extension of the Commutative Property of Multiplication. In effect, you are performing the multiplication as if it reads (4)(3)(w)(w), instead of (4)(w)(3)(w). At the end of the problem, remember <u>not</u> to combine $12w^2$ and $52w$ into a single term, since they are unlike terms.

4

Example: *How is $(-5w^2)(8w + 5)$ written without parentheses?*

Solution: Similar to Example 3, the first operation is $(-5w^2)(8w)$; then do $(-5w^2)(5)$. The answer is $-40w^3 - 25w^2$.

5

Example: *What expression is equivalent to $(2)(3x^2 - 7x + 18)$ without parentheses?*

Solution: The Distributive Law of Multiplication Over Addition and Subtraction can be extended to expressions such as these. The three operations will be $(2)(3x^2)$, $(2)(-7x)$, and $(2)(18)$. The answer is $6x^2 - 14x + 36$.

Let's Review
SEE LESSON 5

6

Example: *What expression is equivalent to $(-9x)(x^3 + 3x^2 - 9)$ without parentheses?*

Solution: Similar to Example 5, the three operations will be $(-9x)(x^3)$, $(-9x)(3x^2)$, and $(-9x)(-9)$. The answer is $-9x^4 - 27x^3 + 81x$.

MathFlash!

Remember that x means x^1, so that a multiplication such as $(-9x)(x^3)$ really means $(-9x^1)(x^3)$. Then the exponents are added to get $-9x^4$.

Example: *What expression is equivalent to (y + 6)(y + 1) without parentheses?*

7

Solution: This looks somewhat different, but stay the course! In multiplications such as these, we need to multiply each part (term) in the first set of parentheses by each term in the second set of parentheses. Our plan will be to do the following multiplications: $(y)(y)$, $(y)(1)$, $(6)(y)$, and then $(6)(1)$. This technique is easy to remember if you think of the word **FOIL**,

Let's Review
SEE LESSON 3

    F = first terms
    O = outer terms
    I = inner terms
    L = last terms

Take a moment to make this association. The four multiplications lead to $y^2 + 1y + 6y + 6$. We are allowed to combine $1y$ and $6y$ to get $7y$. The answer becomes $y^2 + 7y + 6$.

MathFlash!

*Think of the operations in Example 7 as a "double distribution." The y in the first set of parentheses is distributed to each of y and "1" in the second set of parentheses. Then the "6" is distributed to both y and "1" in the second set of parentheses. In reality, the four required multiplications may be performed in <u>any</u> order. However, using the **FOIL** method is an easy way to ensure that you perform <u>all</u> the required multiplications. In any subsequent examples, we will use y in place of 1y, x in place of 1x, z in place of 1z, and so forth.*

Example: *What expression is equivalent to (2y + 3)(–y + 5) without parentheses?*

8

Solution: Using the FOIL method, the <u>f</u>irst terms are $2y$ and $-y$, the <u>o</u>uter terms are $2y$ and 5, the <u>i</u>nner terms are 3 and $-y$, and the <u>l</u>ast terms are 3 and 5. Then, $(2y)(-y) + (2y)(5) + (3)(-y) + (3)(5) = -2y^2 + 10y - 3y + 15$, which simplifies to $-2y^2 + 7y + 15$.

Example: *What expression is equivalent to $(z^2 - 8)(6z - 11)$ without parentheses?*

9

Solution: Using the FOIL method, $(z^2)(6z) + (z^2)(-11) + (-8)(6z) + (-8)(-11) = 6z^3 - 11z^2 - 48z + 88$. This becomes the final answer, since there are no similar terms to be combined.

Example: *What expression is equivalent to $(z^2 + 10)(2z^2 - 9)$ without parentheses?*

10

Solution: Using the FOIL method, $(z^2)(2z^2) + (z^2)(-9) + (10)(2z^2) + (10)(-9) = 2z^4 - 9z^2 + 20z^2 - 90 = 2z^4 + 11z^2 - 90$.
Note that it is important to remember to combine similar terms, namely, $-9z^2$ and $20z^2$.

 Test Yourself!

Perform each multiplication and simplify completely.

1. $(-4)(4x + 1)$ *Answer:* _____

2. $(8y)(3y - 2)$ *Answer:* _____

3. $(-z^2)(10z + 3)$ *Answer:* _____

4. $(5)(w^2 + 11w - 6)$ *Answer:* _____

5. $(-3y)(y^3 + 12y - 5)$ *Answer:* _____

6. $(z + 8)(z - 9)$ *Answer:* _____

7. $(2x - 13)(2x + 7)$

    Answer: _____

8. $(-3w + 4)(-2w + 1)$

    Answer: _____

9. $(4y^2 - 1)(y - 6)$

    Answer: _____

10. $(x^2 + 12)(5x^2 + 2)$

    Answer: _____

Exponents, Multiplication, and Division—Part 3

In this lesson, we will explore the rules of exponents, with respect to division. At this point, you may want to review Examples 6, 7, and 8 and Rule 2 from Lesson 13. Technically, we will only discuss "short" division, which involves only one term in the divisor (denominator of a fraction). Expressions such as x, $8w$, and $-2y^2$ are each considered "one term," whereas an expression such as $3x + 1$ and $z^2 - 6$ are each considered "two terms." Terms are separated by "+" or by "−" signs.

Your Goal: When you have completed this lesson, you will be able to divide algebraic expressions involving short division.

LESSON 15

Exponents, Multiplication, and Division—Part 3

Example: *What expression is equivalent to $\dfrac{6x^2 + 4x}{2}$ in simplest form?*

1

Solution: This is a short division problem, where 2 is the divisor. We simply treat $\dfrac{6x^2 + 4x}{2}$ as if it were two separate fractions, namely, $\dfrac{6x^2}{2}$ and $\dfrac{4x}{2}$. Since $\dfrac{6x^2}{2} = 3x^2$ and $\dfrac{4x}{2} = 2x$, the answer is $3x^2 + 2x$.

For each term in short division problems, divide the associated numbers, followed by applying the rules of division with exponents of like letters. If there were a 5x in place of a 4x in this example, we could write the answer as either $3x^2 + 2.5x$ or $3x^2 + 2\dfrac{1}{2}x$, or even as $3x^2 + \dfrac{5}{2}x$.

Example: *What expression is equivalent to $\dfrac{15y^2 - 40y}{5y}$ in simplest form?*

2

Solution: In this division problem, $5y$ is the divisor, so we rewrite the example as $\dfrac{15y^2}{5y} - \dfrac{40y}{5y}$. Notice that the y's can cancel in the fraction $\dfrac{40y}{5y}$. Now, remember to divide the coefficients and subtract the exponents. You then get the answer of $3y - 8$.

3

Example: *What expression is equivalent to* $\dfrac{54z^3 + 42z^2}{6z}$ *in simplest form?*

Solution: Let's rewrite this division example as $\dfrac{54z^3}{6z} + \dfrac{42z^2}{6z}$. Using the rules

of exponents, we get $9z^2 + 7z$.

(Incidentally, we assume that any letter in the denominator is not zero, since the fraction would not be defined.)

4

Example: *What expression is equivalent to* $\dfrac{5w^4 - 4w^2 + w}{w}$ *in simplest form?*

Solution: Based on what you have seen in Examples 1, 2, and 3, we know

that we can rewrite this example as $\dfrac{5w^4}{w} - \dfrac{4w^2}{w} + \dfrac{w}{w}$. Then, the

result of these three separate divisions will give us the answer of
$5w^3 - 4w + 1$.

The answers to any of these division examples can be checked by
multiplication. Note that $(w)(5w^3 - 4w + 1) = 5w^4 - 4w^2 + w$.

MathFlash!

Be sure that when you cancel out the w's in the last fraction, you use

1 in place of $\dfrac{w}{w}$. Remember that any quantity (except zero) divided

by itself results in 1.

Example:

5

What expression is equivalent to $\dfrac{8x^3 + 6x^2 + 12x}{4x}$ in simplest form?

Solution:

As in Example 4, we rewrite this division as $\dfrac{8x^3}{4x} + \dfrac{6x^2}{4x} + \dfrac{12x}{4x}$. By performing each separate division, we get $2x^2 + 1\dfrac{1}{2}x + 3$. Note that the middle term could also have been written as $1.5x$ or as $\dfrac{3}{2}x$.

Example:

6

What expression is equivalent to $\dfrac{9y^4 - 18y^3 + 60y^2}{12y^2}$ in simplest form?

Solution:

First rewrite the division as $\dfrac{9y^4}{12y^2} - \dfrac{18y^3}{12y^2} + \dfrac{60y^2}{12y^2}$. Note that we must reduce $\dfrac{9}{12}, \dfrac{18}{12}$ and $\dfrac{60}{12}$. We will get the answer of $\dfrac{3}{4}y^2 - \dfrac{3}{2}y + 5$.

MathFlash!

If you have a fraction such as $\dfrac{13x^3}{3x}$ or $\dfrac{8y^2}{9y}$ you don't have to change the numbers, since they share no common factors (that is, no common numbers by which they can be divided). However, the letters must be simplified. So, the respective answers would be $\dfrac{13}{3}x^2$ and $\dfrac{8}{9}y$. Examples such as $\dfrac{4x}{2x^3}$, where the higher exponent is in the denominator, won't be covered in this book.

For 1–9, perform each division and simplify completely.

1. $\dfrac{15x^3 - 6x}{3}$ *Answer:* _____

2. $\dfrac{20x^2 + 45x}{5}$ *Answer:* _____

3. $\dfrac{30x^3 + 20x}{10x}$ *Answer:* _____

4. $\dfrac{16y^4 - 2y}{2y}$ *Answer:* _____

5. $\dfrac{56y^4 - 7y^2}{14y^2}$ *Answer:* _____

6. $\dfrac{6w^2 - 8w - 66}{6}$ *Answer:* _____

7. $\dfrac{3w^4 + 6w^3 - 27w}{9w}$ *Answer:* _____

8. $\dfrac{50z^4 + 90z^3 - 7z^2}{10z^2}$ *Answer:* _____

9. $\dfrac{36z^3 - 24z^2 + 42z}{3z}$ *Answer:* _____

10. **Which one of the following division problems is <u>not</u> covered by the material in this lesson?**

    (A) $\dfrac{5x^2 + 8x}{5}$ (C) $\dfrac{5x^4 + 8x^3 + 14x}{2x}$

    (B) $\dfrac{5x + 8}{5x + 6}$ (D) $\dfrac{5x^3 + 35}{10}$

LESSONS
11-15

QUIZ THREE

1. Which of the following expressions is equivalent to $(y^2 - 8)(2y^2 + 5)$?

    A $2y^4 - 21y^2 - 40$

    B $2y^4 + 21y^2 - 40$

    C $2y^4 + 11y^2 - 40$

    D $2y^4 - 11y^2 - 40$

2. The total cost of 16 gallons of paint, at last week's price of $2.60 per gallon, is the same as the total cost of 19 gallons of paint this week. What is the price for a gallon of paint this week?

    A $2.17

    B $2.19

    C $2.21

    D $2.23

3. In the Pleasant Way School District, the cost of computers per pupil varies directly as the number of computers bought. If the cost per pupil is $56 when 300 computers are bought, what is the cost per pupil if 675 computers are bought?

    A $154.00

    B $140.00

    C $126.00

    D $112.00

4. In using Squeaky Clean laundry detergent, it is recommended that $\frac{3}{8}$ cup of this cleaner be used with each $1\frac{1}{2}$ gallons of water. What fraction of a cup of this cleaner should be used if the clothes to be washed require $2\frac{1}{4}$ gallons of water?

    A $\frac{7}{16}$

    B $\frac{9}{16}$

    C $\frac{3}{4}$

    D $\frac{7}{8}$

5. What is the simplified form for $\frac{(w^3)^4}{w^4}$?

    A w^8

    B w^6

    C w^4

    D w^3

6. In traveling from Houston to Dallas, a bus that averages 55 miles per hour can cover this distance in 262 minutes. Speed varies inversely as time. If the bus were able to average 62 miles per hour, how many minutes would be required to make this same trip?

    A 292

    B 257

    C 232

    D 217

7. **Which expression is equivalent to $\dfrac{24x + 72x^4}{24x}$?**

    A $1 + 3x^3$

    B $1 + 3x^4$

    C $3x^3$

    D $1 + 48x^3$

8. **Which one of the following is equivalent to $(3z - 4)(-5z + 2)$?**

    A $-15z^2 - 26z - 8$

    B $-15z^2 - 14z - 8$

    C $-15z^2 + 14z - 8$

    D $-15z^2 + 26z - 8$

9. **Which expression is equivalent to $\dfrac{16w^2 - 12w^4 + 32w^6}{4w^2}$?**

    A $4 - 3w^2 + 8w^3$

    B $4 - 3w^2 + 8w^4$

    C $4w - 3w^2 + 8w^3$

    D $4w - 3w^2 + 8w^4$

10. **Which one of the following is equivalent to $\dfrac{64^{30}}{64^3}$?**

    A 8^{27}

    B 64^{10}

    C 64^{27}

    D 64^{33}

Factoring with One Variable—Part I

In this lesson, we will explore one method used to factor a given algebraic expression, using a single variable, into two component parts. In reality, factoring can be applied to expressions involving several variables. As we mentioned in Lessons 2 and 3, any letter can be used, but we will use w, x, y, and z in the examples. Factoring an expression involves rewriting it in a multiplication (product) format. For example, 10 can be written as 5×2, and one way of writing 80 is 16×5.

Your Goal: The information you learn in the next few lessons will be vital to your understanding of the methods used to solve equations in Lesson 20. You will see that **factoring is essentially "reverse multiplication," which is really division**.

When you have completed this lesson, you will be able to identify the first factoring technique, as well as perform the operation of factoring.

Factoring with One Variable—Part 1

From Lesson 14, you already know that $4x(x + 6) = 4x^2 + 24x$ and that $(x - 2)(x + 5) = x^2 + 3x - 10$. The process of factoring is really reversing the steps of multiplication of algebraic expressions. In your final answer, each component of the factoring must be a number or an expression that cannot be further factored. The first type of factoring we will learn is called **Common Term Factoring**. This means that we are seeking a common number, letter, or combination of number and letter that is common to all component parts (terms).

1

Example: *What is the factored form of $2x + 8$?*

Solution: In this expression, we can see that 2 is a factor of $2x$ and of 8. To start the factoring process, we write $(2)(\square \ \square)$. Now, we divide each of the parts of $2x + 8$ by 2. Since $2x \div 2 = x$ and $8 \div 2 = 4$. The final answer is $(2)(x + 4)$.

2

Example: *What is the factored form of $x^2 - 9x$?*

Solution: You should be able to spot an x in each of x^2 and $9x$, which means that x is a factor of x^2 and of $9x$. Additionally, from Lesson 13, you know that $(x)(x) = x^2$. Simply divide each of the two parts of the original expression by x to get $x - 9$. The answer is $(x)(x - 9)$.

3

Example: *What is the factored form of $8x^2 + 28$?*

Solution: In this expression, you probably see more than one possible choice that would be a factor of each of $8x^2$ and 28. We just need the greatest common factor, or GCF, of 8 and 28, which is 4.

Since $\frac{8x^2 + 28}{4} = 2x^2 + 7$, the answer is $(4)(2x^2 + 7)$.

We will discuss the rule involving the GCF for numbers and letters in Example 4.

MathFlash!

If you had only selected 2 as the "outside" factor, your answer would have been (2)(4x² + 14). This is not the correct final answer, since 4x² + 14 is further factorable. (It contains a common number, 2.) However, you would arrive at the correct answer if you kept factoring.

4

Example: *What is the factored form of $7x^3 - 21x^2$?*

Solution: Whenever you are looking for a greatest common factor involving the same variable (letter), you only need to identify the <u>lowest</u> exponent. The variable with this exponent becomes part of the greatest common factor.

We know that the GCF of 7 and 21 is 7.

Now we know that the GCF of x^3 and x^2 is x^2. $7x^3 - 2x^2$ can be written as **7xxx − 3•7xx**. The GCF for the original expression becomes $7x^2$. Just divide each of the two parts of $7x^3 - 21x^2$ by $7x^2$ to get $x - 3$. The answer is $(7x^2)(x - 3)$.

5

Example: *What is the factored form of $15y^4 + 40y^2$?*

Solution: The GCF of 15 and 40 is 5, and the GCF of y^4 and y^2 is y^2. So, the GCF for the given expression is $5y^2$. Calculate $\dfrac{15y^4 + 40y^2}{5y^2} =$

$\dfrac{15y^4}{5y^2} + \dfrac{40y^2}{5y^2} = 3y^2 + 8$, so our answer is $(5y^2)(3y^2 + 8)$.

6

Example: *What is the factored form of $9z^2 - 12z + 30z^4$?*

Solution: This expression has three parts (terms), but don't panic! First, look for the GCF of the numbers 9, 12, and 30, which is 3. Can you spot the GCF for z^2, z, and z^4? It would be z. The GCF is $3z$. Dividing each of the three parts of $9z^2 - 12z + 30z^4$ by $3z$ would yield $3z - 4 + 10z^3$.

The answer is $(3z)(3z - 4 + 10z^3)$.

MathFlash!

You can check the accuracy of your answers by using the multiplication rules you learned in Lesson 14 examples 4 and 5.

7

Example: *What is the factored form of $w^4 - 2w^3 - 10w$?*

Solution: Since 1 is the number in front of w^4, we are first looking for the GCF of 1, 2, and 10, which is 1. The number one is invisible in the actual factoring, since it will not change any of the given numbers in the original expression. However, you should note that w is common to all three terms and therefore is the GCF. Now, $\dfrac{w^4 - 2w^3 - 10w}{w} = w^3 - 2w^2 - 10$. This means that the answer is $(w)(w^3 - 2w^2 - 10)$.

8

Example: *What is the factored form of $24y^5 + 18y^4 + 42y^3$?*

Solution: The GCF of 24, 18, and 42 is 6. The GCF of y^5, y^4, and y^3 is y^3. (Remember to take the <u>lowest</u> exponent.) The GCF of the entire expression is $6y^3$. Divide each term of the given expression by $6y^3$ to get $4y^2 + 3y + 7$. The answer is $(6y^3)(4y^2 + 3y + 7)$.

MathFlash!

To factor $10x^2 - 5x$, the GCF to use is $5x$. Divide each of the terms of $10x^2 - 5x$ by $5x$ to get $2x - 1$. Remember that $5x$ divided by $5x$ is 1, <u>not</u> 0.
The answer to the factoring is $(5x)(2x - 1)$.

Test Yourself!

Write the factored form of each of the following expressions.

1. $3y^2 + 12y$ Answer: _____

2. $10x^2 - 25x^3$ Answer: _____

3. $6y + 42y^3$ Answer: _____

4. $w^3 - 4w^2 + 11w$ Answer: _____

5. $20z^2 + 8$ Answer: _____

6. $9y - 54$ Answer: _____

7. $6x^2 - 18x - 33$ Answer: _____

8. $16z^4 - 56z^2$ Answer: _____

9. $7w + 7w^2 + 35w^3$ Answer: _____

10. $12z^4 - 10z + 26z^2$ Answer: _____

Factoring with One Variable—Part 2

In this lesson, we will explore a second method used to factor a given algebraic expression, using a single variable, into two or three component parts. Factoring can be applied to expressions involving several variables. We will continue to use w, x, y, and z in the examples. When faced with a factoring problem, you should first attempt the method you learned in Lesson 16, namely, look for a common factor. This may be a number, letter, or a combination of both.

Your Goal: When you have completed this lesson, you will be able to identify and use one additional factoring technique.

LESSON 17

Factoring with One Variable—Part 2

You already know that $(x - 2)(x + 2) = x^2 + 2x - 2x - 4 = x^2 - 4$ and that $(2y - 3)(2y + 3) = 4y^2 + 6y - 6y - 9 = 4y^2 - 9$.

The expression $x^2 - 4$ can be factored as $(x - 2)(x + 2)$ and that $4y^2 - 9$ can be factored as $(2y - 3)(2y + 3)$. This type of factoring can be labeled as the Difference of Two Squares, and it involves two perfect squares that are separated by a minus sign.

With respect to numbers, you should memorize the following list: 1, 4, 9, 16, 25, 36, 49, 64, 81, and 100. These numbers are the result of evaluating $1^2, 2^2, 3^2, \ldots, 10^2$.

With variables (letters), perfect squares are represented with even exponents. Consider these identities: $x^2 = (x)(x)$, $x^4 = (x^2)(x^2)$, $x^6 = (x^3)(x^3)$. You can see that each of x^2, x^4, and x^6 are all perfect squares, since they are the result of some quantity multiplied by itself.

We can also see why a term such as $25y^2$ is also a perfect square, since $25y^2 = (5y)(5y)$. Can you explain why $49z^6$ is a perfect square? Hopefully, you recognize that $49z^6 = (7z^3)(7z^3)$.

The general form for this type of factoring is usually given as $A^2 - B^2 = (A - B)(A + B)$. To use this factoring method successfully, you need only identify what expressions, namely A and B, are actually being squared.

1

Example: *What is the factored form of $y^2 - 100$?*

Solution: The general form is $A^2 - B^2 = (A - B)(A + B)$. Since $y^2 = (y)(y)$ and $100 = (10)(10)$, we can replace A by y and replace B by 10. The answer is $(y - 10)(y + 10)$.

2

Example: *What is the factored form of $9x^2 - 1$?*

Solution: Since $9x^2 = (3x)(3x)$ and $1 = (1)(1)$, we can replace A by $3x$ and replace B by 1. The answer is $(3x - 1)(3x + 1)$.

3

Example: *What is the factored form of 64 − z⁴?*

Solution: We know that $64 = (8)(8)$ and that $z^4 = (z^2)(z^2)$.
Following the procedure shown in Examples 1 and 2, the answer is
$(8 - z^2)(8 + z^2)$.

MathFlash!

*You may certainly write the previous answer as $(8 + z^2)(8 - z^2)$.
Likewise, you could switch the order of the parentheses for any
examples that use this type of factoring. However, for consistency,
we will place the expression with the negative sign first.*

4

Example: *What is the factored form of −16 + w²?*

Solution: Don't be fooled by this appearance! We can legally rewrite
$-16 + w^2$ as $w^2 - 16$. The signs in front of each term are
unchanged. Now, since $w^2 = (w)(w)$ and $16 = (4)(4)$, the
answer is $(w - 4)(w + 4)$.

5

Example: *What is the factored form of −49x² + 1?*

Solution: Similar to Example 4, let's rewrite $-49x^2 + 1$ as $1 - 49x^2$.
Since $1 = (1)(1)$ and $49x^2 + (7x)(7x)$, the answer is $(1 - 7x)(1 + 7x)$.

6

Example: *What is the factored form of 2x² −50?*

Solution: Looks like we've been thrown a curve ball! We know that this does
not appear to be a difference of two squares, since neither $2x^2$ nor
50 is a perfect square. However we spot a common term (GCF),
namely, 2. Using common term factoring, $2x^2 - 50 = (2)(x^2 - 25)$.

Normally, this would be the end of the problem. But we recognize
that the second set of parentheses represents factoring involving
a difference of two squares. This means that we need to continue
the factoring process by noting that $x^2 - 25 = (x - 5)(x + 5)$. The
final answer is $(2)(x - 5)(x + 5)$.

MathFlash!

Always consider Common Term Factoring before using the Difference of Two Squares Factoring. Had Example 6 been $2x^2 + 50$, the correct factoring would have been $(2)(x^2 + 25)$.

At this point, you <u>cannot</u> use the Difference of Two Squares Factoring because there is a plus sign.

7

Example: *What is the factored form of $80 - 5w^2$?*

Solution: Once again, we must use Common Term Factoring, by recognizing that 5 is a factor of each term. Then $80 - 5w^2 = (5)(16 - w^2)$. Now, looking at $16 - w^2$, we recognize this expression as a difference of two squares. Thus, since $16 - w^2 = (4 - w)(4 + w)$, the final answer is $(5)(4 - w)(4 + w)$.

8

Example: *What is the factored form of $100y - y^3$?*

Solution: Using Common Term Factoring, with y as the common term, $100y - y^3$ becomes $(y)(100 - y^2)$. Now, use Difference of Two Squares Factoring to arrive at the final answer of $(y)(10 - y)(10 + y)$.

9

Example: *What is the factored form of $75w^4 - 3$?*

Solution: The common term of $75w^4 - 3$ is 3, so we get $(3)(25w^4 - 1)$. Now, using the Difference of Two Squares Factoring, $25w^4 = (5w^2)(5w^2)$ and $1 = (1)(1)$. The final answer is $(3)(5w^2 - 1)(5w^2 + 1)$.

10

Example: *What is the factored form of $36z^4 - 9z^2$?*

Solution: This is an example that shows both Common Term Factoring and Difference of Two Squares Factoring at the same time. First use Common Term Factoring to write $36z^4 - 9z^2 = (9z^2)(4z^2 - 1)$. Now, use Difference of Two Squares Factoring to get $4z^2 - 1 = (2z - 1)(2z + 1)$. The final answer is $(9z^2)(2z - 1)(2z + 1)$.

Remember that when you use Common Term Factoring, you must look for the greatest common factor, not just any factor.

11

Example: ***What is the factored form of $81x^3 - 49x^5$?***

Solution: Noting that x^3 is the greatest common factor of these two terms, we rewrite $81x^3 - 49x^5$ as $(x^3)(81 - 49x^2)$, using Common Term Factoring.
Now, using the Difference of Two Squares Factoring, $81 - 49x^2 = (9 - 7x)(9 + 7x)$. The final answer is $(x^3)(9 - 7x)(9 + 7x)$.

12

Example: ***What is the factored form of $10y^4 - 360$?***

Solution: 10 is the common factor, so $10y^4 - 360 = (10)(y^4 - 36)$.
Each of y^4 and 36 is a perfect square, separated by a minus sign, so we can use the Difference of Two Squares Factoring to write $y^4 - 36$ as $(y^2 - 6)(y^2 + 6)$.
The final answer is $(10)(y^2 - 6)(y^2 + 6)$.

Test Yourself!

Write the factored form of each of the following expressions. Stay alert for examples that use both factoring techniques that you have learned.

1. $x^2 - 36$ Answer: _____

2. $49z^2 - 100$ Answer: _____

3. $-4w^4 + 25$ Answer: _____

4. $7w^2 - 567$ Answer: _____

5. $z^3 - 9z$ Answer: _____

6. $x^4 - 4$ Answer: _____

7. $y^6 - 16$ Answer: _____

8. $4x^2 - 36x^4$ Answer: _____

9. $-z^2 + 49$ Answer: _____

10. $60y^5 - 60y^3$ Answer: _____

18

Factoring with One Variable—Part 3

In this lesson, we will explore a third method used to factor a given algebraic expression into two or three component parts. We will use a single variable and will continue to use *w*, *x*, *y*, and *z* in the examples.

When faced with a factoring problem, you should first try the methods you learned in Lessons 16 and 17. The factoring method you will see in this lesson is called Trial and Error Factoring. For all factoring problems, <u>only integers</u> are allowed in the factors.

Your Goal: When you have completed this lesson, you will be able to identify and use an additional factoring technique that involves three terms.

LESSON 18

Factoring with One Variable—Part 3

You have seen how to multiply $y + 6$ by $y + 1$. The product, $y^2 + 7y + 6$, is an expression with three terms.

By the definition of factoring, if you were asked to factor $y^2 + 7y + 6$, your answer would be $(y + 6)(y + 1)$.

Let's Review
SEE
LESSON
14
Ex. 7

The focus of this lesson is to show how to factor a three-term expression whose highest exponent is 2 and whose leading coefficient is 1. Coefficients are the numbers that precede the letters. For example, in the expression $w^3 - 11w^2 + 13w$, the coefficients of w^3, w^2, and w are 1, –11, and 13, respectively.

The number 1 is the leading coefficient for this expression because it is attached to the letter with the highest exponent.

1

Example: *What is the factored form of $x^2 + 8x + 7$?*

Solution: There is no common term, and this cannot be a difference of two squares, since there are three terms. We start out by writing $(x\square)(x\square)$. Since we intend to write two terms in each set of parentheses, which are called binomials, think of the FOIL technique that you used in Lesson 14. In the current example, $x^2 + 8x + 7$, we will have $(x + \square)(x + \square)$, the two blanks will be filled in by two numbers with a sum of 8 and whose product is 7. The numbers 1 and 7 fit both criteria, so the answer is $(x + 1)(x + 7)$. Of course, the answer can be written as $(x + 7)(x + 1)$. Incidentally, notice that the initial two x's are automatic.

Example: *What is the factored form of $y^2 + 6y + 8$?*

2

Solution: The answer will start out as $(y + \square)(y + \square)$. **Note that both 6 and 8 are positive, so both sets of parentheses must contain plus signs.**

The term $6y$ is the result of the outer and inner products, and the number 8 is the product of the two numbers in these blanks.

We have two choices, namely, 1 and 8, or 2 and 4. If you fill in the blanks with 1 and 8, can you see that the result of the sum of the outer and inner products will not be 6 but 9? But, if you use the numbers 2 and 4, you will get 6. The answer is $(y + 2)(y + 4)$.

Example: *What is the factored form of $w^2 - 12w + 11$?*

3

Solution: You can probably see that the answer will start as $(w\square)(w\square)$. The number −12 will be the sum of the outer and inner products, and the number 11 is the product of the two missing numbers that belong in the blanks. The only way to get a product of +11 is either $(+1)(+11)$ or $(-1)(-11)$. Remember that we don't use fractions here. We do not want to use +1 and +11, since we would not get the −12w term. By using −1 and −11, the answer becomes $(w - 1)(w - 11)$. You can check that this is correct by the FOIL method.

Thus far, we have seen that when the example starts as $w^2 + \square\ w + \square$, we want the factored form to appear as $(w + \square)(w + \square)$. When the example starts as $w^2 - \square\ w + \square$, the factored form will appear as $(w - \square)(w - \square)$. Each group of blanks represents numbers. Before we introduce Example 4, consider these two product problems:

    a. $(x - 5)(x + 2) = x^2 - 3x - 10$

    b. $(x - 3)(x + 7) = x^2 + 4x - 21$

Given the expression $x^2 - 3x - 10$, we see that the factored form is $(x - 5)(x + 2)$. If you had to determine the correct factoring, notice that there are two numbers, −5 and +2, that satisfy the conditions that their sum is −3 and their product is −10. Although there are several ways to write two numbers whose sum is −3, and several ways to write two numbers whose product is −10, the numbers −5 and +2 are the <u>only</u> two numbers that do both.

Similarly, $(x - 3)(x + 7)$ is the factored form of $x^2 + 4x - 21$. Notice that the sum of the numbers -3 and $+7$ is $+4$, and their product is -21. You can find several pairs of numbers whose sum is 4, as well as pairs of numbers whose product is -21, but -3 and $+7$ are the <u>only</u> two numbers that do both. Now you can appreciate why this type of factoring is called Trial and Error; among several possible choices, you need to find the single correct choice.

Notice that in each of $x^2 - 3x - 10$ and $x^2 + 4x - 21$, the last number is negative. Thus, you must be sure that your factoring starts as $(x - \square)(x + \square)$.

Example: *What is the factored form of $z^2 - z - 30$?*

4

Solution: The last term is negative, so we start out with $(z - \square)(z + \square)$. We are searching for two numbers whose product is -30 and whose sum is -1. (Remember that $-z$ means $-1z$.) Pairs of numbers whose product is 30 include (a) 1 and 30, (b) 2 and 15, (c) 3 and 10, and (d) 5 and 6. Keep in mind that whichever pair you select, one number will be negative, and the other will be positive. Hopefully, you agree that 5 and 6 would be the correct choice. Also, since their sum must be -1, the correct signs for these numbers would be -6 and $+5$. The answer becomes $(z - 6)(z + 5)$.

At this point, it would be helpful to summarize the assignment of signs to each of the types of Trial and Error Factoring examples that we have seen. Let's use x as the variable, but any letter would serve as well. Each group of blanks represents numbers.

To factor $x^2 + \square x + \square$, use $(x + \square)(x + \square)$.

To factor $x^2 - \square x + \square$, use $(x - \square)(x - \square)$.

To factor $x^2 + \square x - \square$ or $x^2 - \square x - \square$, use $(x - \square)(x + \square)$.

Example: *What is the factored form of $x^2 + 6x - 16$?*

5

Solution: You already know that $(x - \square)(x + \square)$ is the way the answer should appear. The pairs of numbers with a product of 16 are
    (a) 1 and 16
    (b) 2 and 8
    (c) 4 and 4
The winning combination is 2 and 8. Since the middle term of $x^2 + 6x - 16$ is $+6$, we should use -2 and $+8$. The answer is $(x - 2)(x + 8)$.

6

Example: *What is the factored form of $y^2 - 10y + 24$?*

Solution: The answer should appear as $(y - \square)(y - \square)$. The pairs of numbers with a product of 24 are

     (a) 1 and 24
     (b) 2 and 12
     (c) 3 and 8
     (d) 4 and 6

All that is needed at this stage is to find the pair that has a sum of 10. Sure enough, we will use 4 and 6, so the answer is $(y - 4)(y - 6)$.

7

Example: *What is the factored form of $w^2 + 11w - 60$?*

Solution: The answer should appear as $(w - \square)(w + \square)$. The number 60 is a very popular number, since the pairs of numbers we need to consider are (a) 1 and 60, (b) 2 and 30, (c) 3 and 20, (d) 4 and 15, (e) 5 and 12, and (f) 6 and 10. Essentially, you need to spot the one pair for which the <u>difference</u> of the numbers is 11; remember, you are using one positive number and one negative number. Choice (d), 4 and 15, is the right choice, and since the middle term of $w^2 + 11w - 60$ is +11, we should use –4 and +15. The answer is $(w - 4)(w + 15)$.

8

Example: *What is the factored form of $z^2 - 26z - 27$?*

Solution: Similar to Example 7, the answer will appear as $(z - \square)(z + \square)$. The pairs of numbers to consider are (a) 1 and 27, and (b) 3 and 9. The correct selection must involve two numbers whose difference is 26. Choice (b) is the winner, and so we use –27 and +1. The answer is $(z - 27)(z + 1)$.

MathFlash!

With an algebraic expression such as $x^2 + 6x + 9$, the correct factoring is $(x + 3)(x + 3)$. Since the same factor is repeated, you may also write the answer as $(x + 3)^2$.

Likewise, the factoring for $x^2 - 10x + 25$ can be written as either $(x - 5)(x - 5)$ or $(x - 5)^2$.

Test Yourself!

Write the factored form of each of the following expressions.

1. $x^2 + 9x + 20$ *Answer:* _____

2. $y^2 + 3y - 18$ *Answer:* _____

3. $w^2 - 14w + 45$ *Answer:* _____

4. $z^2 - 7z - 30$ *Answer:* _____

5. $x^2 + x - 56$ *Answer:* _____

6. $w^2 - 33w + 32$ *Answer:* _____

7. $z^2 - 9z + 14$ *Answer:* _____

8. $y^2 - 8y - 48$ *Answer:* _____

9. $x^2 - 20x + 99$ *Answer:* _____

10. $w^2 + 10w - 39$ *Answer:* _____

19

Factoring with One Variable—Part 4

In this lesson, we will explore the continuation of the Trial and Error method used to factor a given algebraic expression, which you learned in Lesson 18. As we discussed earlier, when faced with a factoring problem, you should first try the methods you learned in Lessons 16 and 17.

Your Goal: When you have completed this lesson, you will be able to identify and use the Trial and Error Factoring technique in more general problems than those in Lesson 18.

LESSON 19

Factoring with One Variable—Part 4

Let's return to Lesson 14, drill exercise 7. Hopefully, your answer to $(2x - 13)(2x + 7)$ was $4x^2 - 12x - 91$. This means that if we were required to factor $4x^2 - 12x - 91$, the answer, by using factoring, must be $(2x - 13)(2x + 7)$. The key element that makes this factoring difficult is the fact that the leading coefficient (number preceding the x^2) is not 1.

You can see that $4x^2$ is the product of $2x$ and itself, and -91 is $(-13)(+7)$. However, you know that another way to get $4x^2$ is the product of $4x$ and x. Other possible ways to get -91 as a product are $(+13)(-7)$, $(+1)(-91)$, or even $(-1)(+91)$.

Now look at the middle term of the answer, namely, $-12x$. Notice that -12 is not the result of adding or subtracting any two numbers; rather, it is a result of adding the outer and inner terms of the FOIL process that you learned in Lesson 14.
The outer term is $(2x)(+7)$, and the inner term is $(-13)(2x)$. When you combine these products, you get $14x - 26x$, which is $-12x$. No other combination of factoring will yield $4x^2 - 12x - 91$. Let's explain the entire process by using examples.

Example: *What is the factored form of $2y^2 + y - 10$?*

Solution: After realizing that this is not Common Term Factoring or Difference of Two Squares Factoring, we know that the only option left is Trial and Error Factoring. How can we get a product of $2y^2$? Only by using $2y$ and y. We can then begin the factoring as $(2y\square)(y\square)$. The fact that the last term of the algebraic expression is negative (-10) and the middle term is positive ($+1y$) means that within the factoring, we need one plus sign and one minus sign. (We will delay putting in the signs right now.)
In order to get a product of 10, we can use either a combination of 1 and 10 or 5 and 2. Suppose you chose 1 and 10. Then the factoring would appear either as $(2y \square 10)(y \square 1)$ or as $(2y \square 1)(y \square 10)$. Remember that the original expression had no common term. Do you see something wrong with $(2y \square 10)(y \square 1)$ as a possible answer?

Hopefully, you realize that $(2y \square 10)$ <u>does</u> have a common term of 2, so it <u>cannot</u> be a correct answer.

Now look at $(2y \square 1)(y \square 10)$. What would you get for the middle term of $2y^2 + y - 10$ as a result of combining the outer and inner terms? You would have $(2y)(10) = 20y$ and $(1)(y) = y$. One of $20y$ or y must be positive, and the other must be negative. This means that the middle term would be either $19y$ or $-19y$, which is not the desired result.

Now we must use 5 and 2 in the two sets of parentheses. Hopefully, you can appreciate why we should <u>not</u> use $(2y \square 2)(y \square 5)$, since there is a common term of 2 in the first set of parentheses.

Our only hope, for factoring, is that we can set up the answer as $(2y \square 5)(y \square 2)$. Look at the inner and outer terms of the multiplication. You would have $(2y)(2) = 4y$ and $(5)(y) = 5y$. Realizing that either $4y$ or $5y$ must be negative, while the other term is positive, there is a way to join them to create the middle term of $+1$. We must have $-4y$ and $+5y$; this can be accomplished with $(2y + 5)(y - 2)$.

Example: *What is the factored form of $3x^2 - 11x + 8$?*

$\boxed{2}$

<u>Solution</u>:   Note first that since the middle term is negative and the last term is positive, we will need a minus sign between the terms in both parentheses when we use Trial and Error Factoring. (Of course, you should assure yourself that neither Common Term nor Difference of Two Squares Factoring is applicable.) We can start with $(3x - \square)(x - \square)$.

The only way to get a product of 8 is either $(1)(8)$ or $(2)(4)$. If you were to choose $(2)(4)$, your answer would be either $(3x - 4)(x - 2)$ or $(3x - 2)(x - 4)$. Take a moment to convince yourself by combining the outer and inner terms of the multiplication that <u>neither</u> of these would yield the required middle term of $-11x$.

Let's try $(1)(8)$. The two possible answer choices are $(3x - 1)(x - 8)$ or $(3x - 8)(x - 1)$. You should be able to verify which one of these is correct. (Don't flip a coin!) Notice that combining the outer and inner terms of $(3x - 1)(x - 8)$ results in $-24x - 1x = 25x$, which is not the correct middle term. The correct answer is $(3x - 8)(x - 1)$.

Example: *What is the factored form of $6x^2 + 19x + 15$?*

3

Solution: This expression has all pluses, so only addition signs will appear in the factored form. The only way to get $6x^2$ is either $(2x)(3x)$ or $(x)(6x)$, and the only way to get 15 is $(3)(5)$ or $(1)(15)$.

Remember that since we do <u>not</u> have a common term in the original expression, it is <u>not</u> possible to have a common term in either of the sets of parentheses.

These are the possible "matchups":
$$(3x + 1)(2x + 15)$$
$$(3x + 5)(2x + 3)$$
$$(6x + 1)(x + 15)$$
$$(6x + 5)(x + 3)$$
(There were four other possibilities, such as $(6x + 3)(x + 5)$, but they won't work since one of the sets of parentheses contains a common term.)

Notice that each of the four matchups satisfies the requirement of signs, and each of them will yield the correct first and last terms of $6x^2 + 19x + 15$. You need to determine which one of them leads to the correct middle term of $19x$.

Remember that $19x$ is just the sum of the outer and inner terms of the multiplication process. The correct answer is $(3x + 5)(2x + 3)$. $(3x)(3) + (5)(2x) = 9x + 10x = 19x$.

Example: *What is the factored form of $6x^2 + 23x + 15$?*

4

Solution: This should go fast. Since you have already discovered the possibilities from Example 3, you are looking for the one that would lead to a middle term of $23x$. The correct answer is $(6x + 5)(x + 3)$.

5

Example: *What is the factored form of $12w^2 - 8w - 7$?*

Solution: First, recognize that since the last number (–7) is negative, one of the parentheses will contain a plus sign, and the other a minus sign. The difficult part of finding the correct combination rests on the number of factors of 12. The number 7 can only be written in product form as (1)(7). Let's write all six possibilities:

$$(4w \ \square \ 7)(3w \ \square \ 1)$$
$$(4w \ \square \ 1)(3w \ \square \ 7)$$
$$(12w \ \square \ 7)(4w \ \square \ 1)$$
$$(12w \ \square \ 1)(w \ \square \ 7)$$
$$(6w \ \square \ 7)(2w \ \square \ 1)$$
$$(6w \ \square \ 1)(2w \ \square \ 7)$$

Notice that we have temporarily omitted the signs.

If you were considering $(4w \ 7)(3w \ 1)$, the middle term would involve $(4w)(1) = 4w$ and $(7)(3w) = 21w$. One of these products must be negative, and the other positive. As such, it is hoped that you realize that $4w$ and $21w$ <u>cannot</u> be combined to yield $-8w$.

Selecting another wrong combination, $(12w \ \square \ 7)(w \ \square \ 1)$, the middle term would combine $(12w)(1) = 12w$ and $(7)(w) = 7w$. Again, $12w$ and $7w$ cannot be combined to yield $-8w$.

Looking at the other four possibilities, we hope that you can agree that $(6w \ \square \ 7)(2w \ \square \ 1)$ is the correct choice. The outer term in multiplication is $6w$, whereas the inner term is $(7)(2w) = 14w$.

We are attempting to attain a middle term of $-8w$. Since $(6w)(1) - (7)(2w) = 6w - 14w = -8w$, the correct answer is $(6w - 7)(2w + 1)$.

6

Example: *What is the factored form of $3y^2 - 15y + 12$?*

Solution: 3 is a common factor of each term. This means that we must use first use Common Term Factoring to get $(3)(y^2 - 5y + 4)$.

Now we must decide if Difference of Two Squares or Trial and Error Factoring is needed. (Lucky us!) Look at $y^2 - 5y + 4$. If this expression can be factored, we must consider $(y - \square)(y - \square)$. The only numbers whose product is 4 are (1)(4) or (2)(2). It is clear that $(y - 4)(y - 1)$ is the combination that will lead to a middle term of $-5y$ in $y^2 - 5y + 4$. The complete answer is $(3)(y - 4)(y - 1)$.

7

Example: *What is the factored form of $4z^2 + 8z - 32$?*

Solution: We first note that there is a common factor of 4, so we rewrite the example as $(4)(z^2 + 2z - 8)$. Moving on, we need to see if $z^2 + 2z - 8$ can be factored by Trial and Error. Use $(z - \square)(z + \square)$ to determine that the correct numbers to fill in are 4 and 2. Now, we need -2 and $+4$, so that the fill-ins become $(z - 2)(z + 4)$. The final answer is $(4)(z - 2)(z + 4)$.

MathFlash!

For all examples and exercises in this lesson, whenever there is Common Term Factoring, there will also be Trial and Error Factoring. In reality, this is not always the case. For example, $2x^2 + 2x + 10 = (2)(x^2 + x + 5)$, and $x^2 + x + 5$ cannot be factored.

8

Example: *What is the factored form of $10y^2 + 92y + 18$?*

Solution: We spot a common term, namely 2, so let's do the Common Term Factoring to get $(2)(5y^2 + 46y + 9)$. The term $5y^2$ can only be achieved with $(5y)(y)$, and the number 9 is either $(1)(9)$ or $(3)(3)$. Thus, for the expression $5y^2 + 46y + 9$, we must check $(5y + 9)(y + 1)$, $(5y + 1)(y + 9)$, and $(5y + 3)(y + 3)$. Can you choose the "winner" among these three selections?

Hopefully, you chose $(5y + 1)(y + 9)$, since this product will lead to a middle term of $46y$. The final answer is $(2)(5y + 1)(y + 9)$.

9

Example: *What is the factored form of $20w^2 - 40w - 25$?*

Solution: The common term is 5, so rewrite the example, using Common Term Factoring, as $(5)(4w^2 - 8w - 5)$. You know that $4w^2$ can result from either $(2w)(2w)$ or $(4w)(w)$. The number 5 can only result from $(1)(5)$. The factoring for $(4w^2 - 8w - 5)$ must be one of the following:

$$(2w \,\square\, 1)(2w \,\square\, 5)$$
$$(4w \,\square\, 5)(w \,\square\, 1)$$
$$(4w \,\square\, 1)(w \,\square\, 5)$$

Now look for the combination that can produce the middle term of $-8w$. The correct combination is $(2w \,\square\, 1)(2w \,\square\, 5)$, and since we seek $-8w$, we should use $(2w + 1)(2w - 5)$. If necessary, perform the multiplication $(2w + 1)(2w - 5)$ to convince yourself that the product is $(4w^2 - 8w - 5)$.

Finally, our answer to the original question is $(5)(2w + 1)(2w - 5)$.

10

Example: *What is the factored form of $9y^2 + 54y + 81$?*

Solution: There is a common term of 9, so initially we can write $(9)(y^2 + 6y + 9)$.

The factoring of $(y^2 + 6y + 9)$ can only be possible with $(y + \square)(y + \square)$.

The possibilities for a product of 9 are either $(3)(3)$ or $(1)(9)$. You should have no difficulty deciding that $(3)(3)$ is the correct combination.

The answer is $(9)(y + 3)(y + 3)$, which can also be written as $(9)(y + 3)^2$.

<u>Caution</u>: Make sure that the exponent 2 is only applied to $(y + 3)$.

Write the factored form of each of the following expressions. Be sure to check first for a common term.

1. $5x^2 + 18x + 13$ Answer: _____

2. $7w^2 - 28w + 28$ Answer: _____

3. $6z^2 - 7z - 5$ Answer: _____

4. $4y^2 - 20y + 21$ Answer: _____

5. $11w^2 + 77w - 88$ Answer: _____

6. $2z^2 - 13z + 20$ Answer: _____

7. $24x^2 - 6x - 9$ Answer: _____

8. $10w^2 + 61w + 6$ Answer: _____

9. $3x^2 + 20x - 63$ Answer: _____

10. $45z^2 - 60z + 20$ Answer: _____

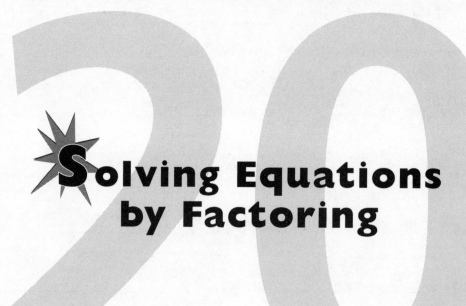

Solving Equations by Factoring

In this lesson, we will utilize all our factoring techniques in order to solve second-degree equations in one variable. The words "second degree" mean that the highest exponent for the variable is 2. It is advised that you review the material that you learned in Lessons 16, 17, 18, and 19 before plunging into this lesson.

Your Goal: When you have completed this lesson, you will be able to solve many (but not all) second-degree equations by using factoring.

LESSON 20

Solving Equations by Factoring

We will begin with an arithmetic fact. Suppose you know that the product of two numbers is zero. If one of the numbers was 3, the other number would be zero. If one of the numbers were –6, the other number would still be zero. In fact, knowing that the first number is <u>not</u> zero would lead us to the conclusion that the second number <u>must</u> be zero. Now, if the first number were zero, is there any conclusion you could reach about the second number? We do not know anything about the second number. In fact, the second number could also be zero. This means that if the product of two numbers is zero, the only conclusion possible is that at least one of these numbers <u>must</u> be zero. Similarly, if the product of three numbers were zero, we could only conclude that at least one of them <u>must</u> be zero.

Algebraically, if $(A)(B) = 0$, where A and B represent any algebraic quantities, at least one of A or B <u>must</u> be zero. By extension, if $(A)(B)(C) = 0$, at least one of A, B, or C <u>must</u> be zero. Remember that "at least" means "one or more." Theoretically, if $(A)(B)(C) = 0$, any two of these or even all three quantities could be zero.

Example: *For what value(s) of x is $x^2 - 25x = 0$?*

1

Solution: Our approach will depend on factoring the left side of the equation. Using Common Term Factoring, x is common to both x^2 and $25x$. We will rewrite the equation as $(x)(x - 25) = 0$. With respect to the preceding paragraph, think of x as replacing A and $x - 25$ as replacing B. We can then say that either $x = 0$ or $x - 25 = 0$.
The first one already states an answer for x. Also, if $x - 25 = 0$, then $x = 25$. Thus, the values of x that we are looking for are 0 or 25.

MathFlash!

Recall that, prior to Example 1, we mentioned that when (A)(B) = 0, at least one of the variables, A or B, must be zero. The possibility existed for both A and B to equal zero (at the same time). For all the second- degree equations in this Workbook, there will be only one variable. Thus, it will not be possible for the quantities representing A and B to be zero at the same time. In Example 1, x can be 0, or x can be 25, but x cannot be both 0 and 25 at the same time.

2

Example: *For what value(s) of y is $8y^2 + 4y = 0$?*

Solution: Common Term Factoring leads to $(4y)(2y + 1) = 0$. If $4y = 0$, then $y = 0$. If $2y + 1 = 0$, then $y = -\frac{1}{2}$. The answers are 0 or $-\frac{1}{2}$. Hopefully, you had no difficulty in solving $2y + 1 = 0$; however, you should review Lessons 2 and 3 if the answer of $-\frac{1}{2}$ does not seem clear.

Let's Review SEE LESSONS 2 & 3

3

Example: *For what value(s) of z is $4z^2 - 1 = 0$?*

Solution: Using the Difference of Two Squares Factoring, $[A^2 - B^2 = (A + B)(A - B)]$, we rewrite this equation as $(2z - 1)(2z + 1) = 0$. If $2z - 1 = 0$, then $z = \frac{1}{2}$. If $2z + 1 = 0$, then $z = -\frac{1}{2}$. The answers are $\frac{1}{2}$ or $-\frac{1}{2}$.

4

Example: *For what value(s) of w is $9w^2 + 6w + 1 = 0$?*

Solution: Using Trial and Error Factoring, let's rewrite this equation as $(3w + 1)(3w + 1) = 0$. We have "twins" in this example (the same binomial multiplied by itself), so we are only solving $3w + 1 = 0$ for w once. The only answer is $w = -\frac{1}{3}$.

MathFlash!

The above is an example of a second-degree equation that contains only one answer. Most second-degree equations contain two answers.

Example: *For what value(s) of x is $x^2 + 4x = 21$?*

5

Solution: Don't get confused! We start out by subtracting 21 from each side, so as to rewrite the equation as $x^2 + 4x - 21 = 0$. Using Trial and Error Factoring, we can write $(x - 3)(x + 7) = 0$. If $x - 3 = 0$, then $x = 3$. If $x + 7 = 0$, then $x = -7$. The answers are 3 or −7.

MathFlash!

If the original second-degree equation does not have zero on one side, you have to perform the operation(s) necessary so that all nonzero terms appear on the same side of the equation. A zero will be placed on the opposite side.

Example: *For what value(s) of y is $3y^2 + 7y + 4 = 0$?*

6

Solution: Using Trial and Error Factoring, we rewrite the equation as

$(3y + 4)(y + 1) = 0$.

If $3y + 4 = 0$, $3y = -4$, then $y = -\dfrac{4}{3}$.

If $y + 1 = 0$, $y = -1$.

The answers are $-\dfrac{4}{3}$ or −1.

7

Example: *For what value(s) of z is $2z^2 - 8z = 24$?*

Solution: Rewrite this equation as $2z^2 - 8z - 24 = 0$. Since 2 is a common term, use Common Term Factoring to get $(2)(z^2 - 4z - 12) = 0$. Next use Trial and Error Factoring on $z^2 - 4z - 12$, which is $(z - 6)(z + 2)$. This gives us $(2)(z - 6)(z + 2) = 0$. If $(A)(B)(C) = 0$, then at least one of these variables must be zero. But, can $2 = 0$? Of course not. If $z - 6 = 0$, then $z = 6$. If $z + 2 = 0$, then $z = -2$. The answers are 6 or –2.

MathFlash!

Whenever you can factor out a number without a variable in these types of equations, you can effectively "drop" the number. That is, ignore it in solving for x. It will not disrupt finding the solutions. Be careful, though, that you do not drop variables. Looking back at Example 2, we did not drop the term 4y. Had we mistakenly dropped 4y, we would have overlooked the answer of zero.

8

Example: *For what value(s) of x is $20x^2 + 8x - 64 = 0$?*

Solution: Since 4 is a common term, let's rewrite the equation as $(4)(5x^2 + 2x - 16) = 0$. At this point, you can simply ignore the number 4 since $4 \neq 0$. Then we have $5x^2 + 2x - 16 = 0$. Using Trial and Error Factoring (and some patience!), you should be able to arrive at $(5x - 8)(x + 2) = 0$. If $5x - 8 = 0$, then $x = \frac{8}{5}$. If $x + 2 = 0$, then $x = -2$. The answers are $\frac{8}{5}$ or –2.

9

Example: *For what value(s) of y is 12w² – 102w + 180 = 0?*

Solution: Don't be intimidated by the large numbers! The number 6 is the greatest common factor, so we can rewrite the equation as $(6)(2x^2 - 17w + 30) = 0$. We will drop the 6, so we can concentrate on factoring $2x^2 - 17w + 30$. After you set up the factoring as $(2w - \square)(w - \square)$, your objective is to find the proper combination (and placement) of the factors of 30. To make life easier for you, remember that since $2x^2 - 17w + 30$ has no common factor, each of $(2w - \square)$ and $(w - \square)$ must <u>not</u> contain a common factor. This hint will limit the choices to the following: $(2w - 1)(w - 30)$, $(2w - 15)(w - 2)$, $(2w - 3)(w - 10)$, or $(2w - 5)(w - 6)$. You only need to find the combination for which the sum of the inner and outer terms of the multiplication will yield $-17w$. The right combination is $(2w - 5)(w - 6)$. Then $2w - 5 = 0$ leads to $w = \frac{5}{2}$, and $w - 6 = 0$ leads to $w = 6$. The two answers are $\frac{5}{2}$ or 6.

MathFlash!

Example 9 was intense, but you had the opportunity to appreciate many pieces of information that you have learned about factoring. In particular, since $2w^2 - 17w + 30$ has no common factors, you would eliminate from consideration a combination such as $(2w - 10)(w - 3)$. This is because $2w - 10$ has a common factor of 2.

10

Example: *For what value(s) of y is 13y² – 33 = 28y?*

Solution: Rewrite the example as $13y^2 - 28y - 33 = 0$. The four possible combinations, without placing any signs, are $(13y \, \square \, 1)(y \, \square \, 33)$, $(13y \, \square \, 33)(y \, \square \, 1)$, $(13y \, \square \, 3)(y \, \square \, 11)$, $(13y \, \square \, 11)(y \, \square \, 3)$. Write down all inner and outer products of these four combinations, bearing in mind that in your final selection, you will need one plus sign and one minus sign. Hopefully, you agree that the last combination is the winning one. The correct factoring for the equation becomes

$(13y + 11)(y - 3) = 0$. The answers are $y = -\frac{11}{13}$ or $y = 3$.

Using factoring techniques, solve each of the following equations.

1. $y^2 - y = 30$

    Factoring: _____   Answer(s): _____

2. $12x^2 - 75 = 0$

    Factoring: _____   Answer(s): _____

3. $w^2 - 14w = 0$

    Factoring: _____   Answer(s): _____

4. $6x^2 - 23x + 15 = 0$

    Factoring: _____   Answer(s): _____

5. $2z^2 + 18z = 44$

    Factoring: _____   Answer(s): _____

6. $9y^2 + 78y + 48 = 0$

    Factoring: _____   Answer(s): _____

7. $7x^2 - 16x + 9 = 0$

    Factoring: _____   Answer(s): _____

8. $4w^2 + 56w + 196 = 0$

    Factoring: _____   Answer(s): _____

9. $15y^2 - 9y = 0$

    Factoring: _____   Answer(s): _____

10. $5z^2 - 42z = 27$

    Factoring: _____   Answer(s): _____

LESSONS
16-20

QUIZ FOUR

1. **What values of *w* satisfy the equation $3w^2 + 6w = 189$?**

    A –9 and 7

    B –9 and –7

    C 9 and –7

    D 9 and 7

2. **What is the factored form of $y^2 - 8y - 84$?**

    A $(y - 6)(y + 14)$

    B $(y - 14)(y + 6)$

    C $(y - 7)(y + 12)$

    D $(y - 12)(y + 7)$

3. **What is the factored form of $2z^3 - 18z^2 + 6z$?**

    A $(2z)(z^3 - 9z + 3)$

    B $(2)(z^3 - 9z + 3)$

    C $(2)(z^2 - 9z + 3)$

    D $(2z)(z^2 - 9z + 3)$

4. **What is the factored form of $20x^2 - 87x + 28$?**

    A $(5x - 4)(4x - 7)$

    B $(20x - 7)(x - 4)$

    C $(10x - 7)(2x - 4)$

    D $(20x - 1)(x - 28)$

5. **What is the complete factored form of $6w^2 + 54w + 120$?**

    A $(6)(w^2 + 9w + 20)$

    B $(3)(2w^2 + 18w + 40)$

    C $(6)(w + 5)(w + 4)$

    D $(6)(w + 10)(w + 2)$

6. **What is the complete factored form of $25x^3 - 16x$?**

    A $(x)(25x^2 - 16)$

    B $(x)(25x - 16)(x + 1)$

    C $(x)(5x - 4)(5x + 4)$

    D $(x)(5x - 4)(5x - 4)$

7. **What values of *y* satisfy the equation $18y^2 - 3y = 0$?**

    A 0 or 6

    B 0 or –6

    C 0 or $-1\frac{1}{6}$

    D 0 or $\frac{1}{6}$

8. **Which one of the following does not factor by the Trial and Error method?**

    A $4w^2 - 4w - 4$

    B $x^2 + x - 6$

    C $y^2 - 3y - 4$

    D $2z^2 + 7z + 3$

9. Which one of the following can be factored using the Difference of Two Squares method?

   A $4w^2 - 16w$

   B $25x - 25y$

   C $100y^2 - 9$

   D $49z^2 - 7z$

10. What is the greatest common factor of $30x^3$ and $18x^4$?

   A $6x^3$

   B $6x^4$

   C $3x^3$

   D $3x^4$

21

Solving Equations by the Quadratic Formula

In this lesson, we will explore a way to solve second-degree equations when factoring is not possible. An example would be the equation $x^2 + 6x + 2 = 0$. None of the factoring techniques that you have learned would be usable here, even though there are real number answers.

Your Goal: When you have completed this lesson, you will be able to solve second-degree equations by using a special formula.

LESSON 21

Solving Equations by the Quadratic Formula

Given a second-degree equation in x, which appears as $Ax^2 + Bx + C = 0$, where A, B, and C represent any real numbers, the **Quadratic Formula** states that the answer(s) for x are found by calculating the value of $\dfrac{-B - \sqrt{B^2 - 4AC}}{2A}$ and $\dfrac{-B + \sqrt{B^2 - 4AC}}{2A}$.

This formula works even if the left side of the equation can be factored. Let's also remind ourselves that any variable can be used; however, we will continue to use one of w, x, y, and z in each equation.

Example: *For what approximate values of x is $x^2 + 6x + 2 = 0$?*

1

Solution: Recall that x^2 means $1x^2$. In this example, $A = 1$, $B = 6$, and $C = 2$.

One answer is found by calculating $\dfrac{-B - \sqrt{B^2 - 4AC}}{2A}$. This becomes

$\dfrac{-6 - \sqrt{6^2 - (4)(1)(2)}}{(2)(1)}$, which simplifies to $\dfrac{-6 - \sqrt{36 - 8}}{2} = \dfrac{-6 - \sqrt{28}}{2}$.

Since we want approximate values, we will determine $\sqrt{28}$ to the nearest thousandth, then round off the final answer to the nearest hundredth.

Now, $\sqrt{28} \approx 5.292$, and so $\dfrac{-6 - \sqrt{28}}{2} \approx \dfrac{-6 - 5.292}{2} = \dfrac{-11.292}{2} \approx -5.65$.

The second answer is found by calculating $\dfrac{-B + \sqrt{B^2 - 4AC}}{2A}$.

This becomes $\dfrac{-6 + \sqrt{6^2 - (4)(1)(2)}}{(2)(1)}$, which simplifies to

$\dfrac{-6 + \sqrt{36 - 8}}{2} = \dfrac{-6 + \sqrt{28}}{2}$. Using 5.292 again as the approximate

value of $\sqrt{28}$, $\dfrac{-6 + \sqrt{28}}{2} \approx \dfrac{-6 + 5.292}{2} = \dfrac{-0.708}{2} \approx -0.35$. Our two

answers are −5.65 or −0.35, rounded off to the nearest hundredth.

The two answers, $\dfrac{-B - \sqrt{B^2 - 4AC}}{2A}$ and $\dfrac{-B + \sqrt{B^2 - 4AC}}{2A}$, are commonly

written as $\dfrac{-B \pm \sqrt{B^2 - 4AC}}{2A}$. The symbol $\pm$ means that the quantity

that follows will be calculated using each of the $-$ and $+$ signs. For
example, if you were to calculate 5 ± 4.2, you would calculate
$5 - 4.2$ or $5 + 4.2$. Your two answers would be 0.8 or 9.2.
For all future examples in this lesson, we will use the expression

$\dfrac{-B \pm \sqrt{B^2 - 4AC}}{2A}$ to calculate the answers. Just be careful to look at

the entire numerator before you divide by the quantity 2A.

(Each of the examples will have two answers.)

2

Example: *For what approximate values of y is $y^2 - 3y - 7 = 0$?*

Solution: First, note that $A = 1$, $B = -3$, and $C = -7$ for the Quadratic Formula.

The two answers are calculated by substituting into $\dfrac{-B \pm \sqrt{B^2 - 4AC}}{2A}$,

which becomes $\dfrac{-(-3) \pm \sqrt{(-3)^2 - (4)(1)(-7)}}{(2)(1)}$. Before we move on,

make <u>absolutely sure</u> that you understand the substitutions that
were just made.

The next step would be $\dfrac{3 \pm \sqrt{9 - (-28)}}{2} = \dfrac{3 \pm \sqrt{37}}{2}$.

Be sure that you realize that $(-3)^2 = +9$ and that $9 - (-28) = 9 + 28$.
Continuing, we will use 6.083 as the approximate value of $\sqrt{37}$.

This can be written as $\sqrt{37} \approx 6.083$. Then $\dfrac{3 \pm \sqrt{37}}{2} \approx \dfrac{3 \pm 6.083}{2}$.

Using the minus sign, the first answer is $\dfrac{3 - 6.083}{2} = \dfrac{-3.083}{2} \approx -1.54$.

Using the plus sign, the second answer is $\dfrac{3 + 6.083}{2} = \dfrac{9.083}{2} \approx 4.54$.

MathFlash!

Every so often, you should check your answer by direct substitution into the original equation. For equations that require the Quadratic Formula, the answers will not normally be exact, but they will be <u>very</u> close. Let's check the answer of 4.54 from Example 2. By substitution into the left side of the original equation, we have $(4.54)^2 - (3)(4.54) - 7 = 20.6116 - 13.62 - 7 = -0.0084$. Although this number is not exactly zero, it is extremely close to zero.

Example: *For what approximate values of z is $z^2 + 4z = 10$?*

3

Solution: Do not use the Quadratic Formula until you rearrange this equation to read as $z^2 + 4z - 10 = 0$. We know that $A = 1$, $B = 4$, and $C = -10$.

By substitution, we get $\dfrac{-4 \pm \sqrt{4^2 - 4(1)(-10)}}{(2)(1)}$.

Further simplification leads to $\dfrac{-4 \pm \sqrt{16 - (-40)}}{2} = \dfrac{-4 \pm \sqrt{56}}{2}$.

Since $\sqrt{56} \approx 7.483$, one answer is $\dfrac{-4 - 7.483}{2} = \dfrac{-11.483}{2} \approx -5.74$.

The second answer is $\dfrac{-4 + 7.483}{2} = \dfrac{3.483}{2} \approx 1.74$.

Example: *For what approximate values of w is $3w^2 - 9w + 1 = 0$?*

4

Solution: In this example, $A = 3$, $B = -9$, and $C = 1$.

By substitution, we get $\dfrac{-(-9) \pm \sqrt{(-9)^2 - (4)(3)(1)}}{(2)(3)}$.

Upon simplifying, we have $\dfrac{9 \pm \sqrt{81 - 12}}{6} = \dfrac{9 \pm \sqrt{69}}{6}$.

Since $\sqrt{69} \approx 8.307$, one answer is $\dfrac{9 - 8.307}{6} = \dfrac{0.693}{6} \approx 0.12$.

The second answer is $\dfrac{9 + 8.307}{6} = \dfrac{17.307}{6} \approx 2.88$.

Example: *For what approximate values of x is –2x² + 12 = 11x?*

Solution: Rewrite the equation as $-2x^2 - 11x + 12 = 0$. See that $-11x$ has been moved to the middle of the three terms on the left side of the equation. $A = -2$, $B = -11$, and $C = 12$.

By substitution, we get $\dfrac{-(-11) \pm \sqrt{(-11)^2 - (4)(-2)(12)}}{(2)(-2)}$.

Watching how you deal with the minus signs, this simplifies to $\dfrac{11 \pm \sqrt{121 - (-96)}}{-4}$, which becomes $\dfrac{11 \pm \sqrt{217}}{-4}$.

Using 14.731 as the approximate value of $\sqrt{217}$,

one answer is $\dfrac{11 - 14.731}{-4} = \dfrac{-3.731}{-4} \approx 0.93$.

The second answer is $\dfrac{11 + 14.731}{-4} = \dfrac{25.731}{-4} \approx -6.43$.

Example: *For what approximate values of w is 5w² = –21w – 15?*

Solution: First, rewrite this equation as $5w^2 + 21w + 15 = 0$.
Now, $A = 5$, $B = 21$, and $C = 15$. Substitute into the Quadratic Formula, to get $\dfrac{-21 \pm \sqrt{(21)^2 - (4)(5)(15)}}{(2)(5)}$.

This simplifies to $\dfrac{-21 \pm \sqrt{441 - 300}}{10} = \dfrac{-21 \pm \sqrt{141}}{10}$.

Using 11.874 as the approximate value of $\sqrt{141}$, one answer is

$\dfrac{-21 - 11.874}{10} = \dfrac{-32.874}{10} \approx -3.29$.

The second answer is $\dfrac{-21 + 11.874}{10} = \dfrac{-9.126}{10} \approx -0.91$.

7

Example: *For what approximate values of z is $10z^2 + 80z - 220 = 0$?*

Solution: You could use the Quadratic Formula substitution immediately, but take another look at this equation. We can reduce (legally) the size of these numbers by effectively dividing by a common number (GCF). In this example, let's divide the equation by 10 to get $z^2 + 8z - 22 = 0$. Now, $A = 1$, $B = 8$, and $C = -22$.

Using the Quadratic Formula, we get $\dfrac{-8 \pm \sqrt{8^2 - (4)(1)(-22)}}{(2)(1)}$,

which becomes $\dfrac{-8 \pm \sqrt{64 + 88}}{2} = \dfrac{-8 \pm \sqrt{152}}{2}$. Since $\sqrt{152} \approx 12.329$,

one answer is $\dfrac{-8 - 12.329}{2} = \dfrac{-20.329}{2} \approx -10.16$.

The second answer is $\dfrac{-8 + 12.329}{2} = \dfrac{4.329}{2} \approx 2.16$.

MathFlash!

In the previous example, you certainly could have used $A = 10$, $B = 80$, and $C = -220$ in the Quadratic Formula.
Your final answers should be exactly the same as we found by using a "reduced" equation.

8

Example: *For what approximate values of y is $16y^2 - 200y + 120 = 0$?*

Solution: Determine that 8 is a common factor of each of 16, 200, and 120. (If you have trouble finding this number, start out by dividing each number by 2, since all three numbers are even.) After dividing the equation by 8, we get $2y^2 - 25y + 15 = 0$. Since the left side of the equation cannot be factored, we must use the Quadratic Formula. $A = 2$, $B = -25$, and $C = 15$. By substitution, we get

$$\dfrac{-(-25) \pm \sqrt{(-25)^2 - (4)(2)(15)}}{(2)(2)} = \dfrac{25 \pm \sqrt{625 - 120}}{4} = \dfrac{25 \pm \sqrt{505}}{4}.$$

Since $\sqrt{505} \approx 22.472$, one answer is $\dfrac{25 - 22.472}{4} = \dfrac{2.528}{4} \approx 0.63$.

The second answer is $\dfrac{25 + 22.472}{4} = \dfrac{47.472}{4} \approx 11.87$.

If you go to check your answers and substitute either of these numbers into the original equation, the left side will be about 0.35. Do not worry too much about this size "error," which happens often when dealing with square roots of large numbers.

MathFlash!

The Quadratic Formula works on equations, even when factoring can be applied. We will use Example 6 from Lesson 20 to illustrate. The equation reads $3y^2 + 7y + 4 = 0$. By direct substitution, we get

$$\frac{-7 \pm \sqrt{7^2 - (4)(3)(4)}}{(2)(3)} = \frac{-7 \pm \sqrt{49 - 48}}{(2)(3)} = \frac{-7 \pm 1}{6}. \text{ One answer is } \frac{-7 - 1}{6} =$$

$-\dfrac{8}{6}$, *which reduces to* $-\dfrac{4}{3}$. *The second answer is* $\dfrac{-7 + 1}{6} = -\dfrac{6}{6}$, *which reduces to –1. These are the same answers as we obtained in Lesson 20, using Trial and Error Factoring.*

Test Yourself!

Using the Quadratic Formula, solve each of the following equations. Show the substitution of values for A, B, and C in the Quadratic Formula. Your answers should be rounded off to the nearest hundredth. Be sure that all terms are on the left side of the equation.

1. $y^2 - 12y - 5 = 0$

    Quadratic Formula: _____ **Answer(s):** _____

2. $x^2 + 18x = 11$

    Quadratic Formula: _____ **Answer(s):** _____

Test Yourself! (continued)

3. $w^2 + 9w + 10 = 0$

    Quadratic Formula: _____   *Answer(s):* _____

4. $15z^2 - 105z + 60 = 0$

    Quadratic Formula: _____   *Answer(s):* _____

5. $4x^2 + 5x - 17 = 0$

    Quadratic Formula: _____   *Answer(s):* _____

6. $2w^2 + 9 = 13w$

    Quadratic Formula: _____   *Answer(s):* _____

7. $18y^2 - 6y - 54 = 0$

    Quadratic Formula: _____   *Answer(s):* _____

8. $100z^2 + 40z = 80$

    Quadratic Formula: _____   *Answer(s):* _____

9. $-3x^2 + 19x - 10 = 0$

    Quadratic Formula: _____   *Answer(s):* _____

10. $20w^2 + 10w - 15 = 0$

    Quadratic Formula: _____   *Answer(s):* _____

22

Solving a System of Linear Equations in Two Variables

In this lesson, we will explore a way to solve two linear equations in two variables. Remember that the word "linear," as applied to equations, means that the highest exponent is 1. Most examples will have exactly one pair of answers. Also, we will inspect systems of equations with either no answers or an indefinite number of answers. The letters for variables that we will use are w, x, y, and z. Keep in mind that any letters are permitted.

Your Goal: When you have completed this lesson, you will be able to determine the nature of the answers to a given system of linear equations.

LESSON 22

Solving a System of Linear Equations in Two Variables

Suppose you were given the equation $x + y = 10$. This is a linear equation in two variables, namely x and y. The equation states that the sum of x and y is 10. If the value of x were 2, then the value of y would be 8. But can x have other values?

Yes, we could assign x the value of 9, then y would equal 1. Theoretically, you could even assign x a value of –3. If $x = -3$, then $y = 13$. In fact, unless otherwise stated, x might even have a value of a fraction or decimal. So, if $x = 6\frac{1}{2}$, then $y = 3\frac{1}{2}$. If you assign the value of 9.9 to x, then you would have to assign the value of 0.1 to y.

For this equation, there is really no specific set of values that must be assigned to x and y.

Once you assign a value to x, then there will automatically be a specific value for y.

> For example, with $2x + 3y = 30$, you first decide on a value for x.
> Then, you find the y value.
> If you decide that x will be 3, the equation would become $(2)(3) + 3y = 30$.
> The value of y would be 8.
> If you made $x = -6$, the equation would be $(2)(-6) + 3y = 30$.
> The value of y becomes 14.

In this instance, y is considered the dependent variable, and x is the independent variable. The opposite would also be true. This would happen whenever you have an equation with two variables.

Let's look at an example containing two linear equations, each with x and y: $x + y = 12$ and $x - y = 4$. We are looking for <u>one</u> value of x and <u>one</u> value of y so that they represent the answers (solutions) for <u>both</u> equations.

> Looking at just the first equation, we could let $x = 10$ and $y = 2$. However, would these values work for the second equation? Absolutely not, unless you had adopted a new number system in which $10 - 2 = 4$!

Incidentally, if you happened to assign a value of 8 to *x* and a corresponding value of 4 to *y* in the first equation, you would have been pleasantly surprised that *x* = 8 and *y* = 4 also works for the second equation. Now, let's develop an algebraic method that removes the guesswork.

Example: *What values of x and y satisfy the system* $\begin{array}{l} x + y = 12 \\ x - y = 4 \end{array}$ *?*

1

Solution: When equals are added to equals the results are equal.

$$
\begin{array}{r}
x + y = 12 \\
x - y = \ 4 \\
\hline
2x + 0 = 16 \\
x = 8
\end{array}
$$

Let's add the two given equations. To find the value of *y*, we can replace this *x* value into either equation. By substitution into the first equation, 8 + *y* = 12. Thus, *y* = 4. This set of values will also work in the second equation.

MathFlash!

Every so often, you should check that your answers do work in both equations. If the pair of answers only satisfies one equation, it is <u>not</u> considered to be a solution to the system of equations.

Example: *What values of x and y satisfy the system* $\begin{array}{l} x + y = 6 \\ 2x - y = 21 \end{array}$ *?*

2

Solution: Once again, we should add these equations:

$$
\begin{array}{r}
x + y = \ 6 \\
2x - y = 21 \\
\hline
3x + 0 = 27 \\
x = 9
\end{array}
$$

Let's substitute this value of *x* into the first equation.
Then we have 9 + *y* = 6, so *y* = –3.
As a check, substitute *x* = 9 and *y* = –3 into the second equation.
Then, (2)(9) – (–3) = 21, which is true.

3

Example: *What values of x and y satisfy the system* $\begin{array}{l}4x + y = 18 \\ 2x + y = 17\end{array}$ *?*

Solution: If you simply add these equations, you will get $6x + 2y = 35$. This equation is correct, but we still don't know what x and y are! Subtracting the second equation from the first equation:

$$
\begin{array}{r}
4x + y = \ 18 \\
-2x - y = -17 \\
\hline
2x \quad\ \ = \ \ 1 \\
x = \dfrac{1}{2}
\end{array}
$$

Let's substitute this value of x into the second equation. Then $(2)\left(\dfrac{1}{2}\right) + y = 17$, so $1 + y = 17$, which leads to $y = 16$.

MathFlash!

If you get an answer that is a fraction, you may also write its decimal equivalent. So, we could have written $x = 0.5$ in example 3. If you get a fractional answer, such as $\dfrac{1}{3}$ or $\dfrac{2}{7}$, you may use the rounded-off decimal equivalent (0.33 and 0.29) as the final answer. However, the corresponding value for y may differ slightly when you substitute into both original equations due to rounding-off.

For the examples in this lesson, we will use the decimal equivalent if it is exact. Otherwise, we will use the fraction.

4

Example: *What values of x and y satisfy the system* $\begin{matrix} 5x - 7y = -1 \\ 5x + 3y = 11 \end{matrix}$ *?*

Solution: Adding these equations leads to $10x - 4y = 10$. This is not a help in solving for x and y. However, if you subtract the second equation from the first equation, you get

$$
\begin{array}{r}
5x - 7y = {-1} \\
-5x - 3y = -11 \\
\hline
-10y = -12 \\
y = \dfrac{12}{10} = \dfrac{6}{5} \text{ or } 1.2
\end{array}
$$

Substitute 1.2 into the second equation to get $(5)(x) + (3)(1.2) = 11$, which becomes $5x + 3.6 = 11$. Then $5x = 7.4$, so $x = 1.48$.

Had the value of x extended beyond two decimal places, we could have just rounded off the answer or used the corresponding reduced fraction. To check these answers in the first equation, substitute 1.48 for x and 1.2 for y.

5

Example: *What values of w and z satisfy the system* $\begin{matrix} w - z = 3 \\ -3w + 2z = -1 \end{matrix}$ *?*

Solution: To add a little spice to our examples, we changed x and y to w and z, but the process is the same. By adding these equations, we get $-2w + z = 2$. By subtracting the second equation from the first equation, we get $w - (-3w) = 4w$, $-z - (2z) = -3z$, and $3 - (-1) = 4$. This leads to $4w - 3z = 4$.

It looks as if we can't proceed any further. Fortunately, we do have another approach. We will use the concept that "when equals are multiplied by equals, the results are equal." This is easily verified.

Let's multiply the first equation by 2 then add equations. It will then appear as $2w - 2z = 6$. Here is how the system now looks:

$$
\begin{array}{r}
2w - 2z = 6 \\
-3w + 2z = -1 \\
\hline
-w = 5
\end{array}
$$

So $w = -5$.

Substitute this value into the first equation to get $-5 - z = 3$. Finally, $z = -8$.

MathFlash!

Looking back at the solution to Example 5, you can see that we arranged for the coefficients (numbers preceding the letters) of one of the variables to be "opposites" of each other. In this way, when the equations are added, only one variable remains. Basically, one of the variables will "drop out" or cancel since they equal zero. If you had wanted to force the w's to drop out in Example 5, you would have multiplied the first equation by 3. Use this approach to do Example 5 again.

6

Example: *What values of w and z satisfy the system $\begin{array}{l} 12w + 2z = 5 \\ 4w + 3z = 9 \end{array}$?*

Solution: Simply adding or subtracting these equations will not "eliminate" either variable. By adding the equations, we get $16w + 5z = 14$. By subtracting the second equation from the first equation, we get $8w - z = -4$. You can force the second equation to have 12 as the coefficient of w by multiplying the second equation by 3 to get $12w + 9z = 27$.

Now, subtract the equations.

$$\begin{array}{r} 12w + 2z = 5 \\ -12w - 9z = -27 \\ \hline -7z = -22 \end{array}$$

$$\text{So } z = \frac{22}{7}.$$

Use the first equation to find the value of w. Substitute to get $12w + (2)\left(\dfrac{22}{7}\right) = 5$, which can be written as $12w + \dfrac{44}{7} = 5$. Multiplying the entire equation by 7 yields $84w + 44 = 35$. Then $84w = -9$, so $w = -\dfrac{9}{84}$, which reduces to $-\dfrac{3}{28}$.

MathFlash!

*These answers in Example 6 were not the most friendly fractions!
Your mathematics instructor may allow you to simply use the
decimal equivalents as answers. In that case, $w \approx -0.11$ and $z \approx 3.14$.
Just be aware that these answers will not completely check the
equations (but they will be close).*

7

Example: *What values of w and z satisfy the system* $\begin{array}{l} 7w + 5z = 21 \\ 3w - 20z = -22 \end{array}$ *?*

Solution: Neither adding these equations nor subtracting them will result in either variable being "dropped." Look carefully at the coefficients of each variable. One of the coefficients of z (5) divides into the other (20), so you can multiply the first equation by 4. This changes the first equation to $28w + 20z = 84$. Now the system of equations becomes:

$$\begin{array}{r} 28w + 20z = 84 \\ \underline{3w - 20z = -22} \\ 31w = 62 \end{array}$$

So $w = 2$.

Use the equation $3w - 20z = -22$ to find the value of z. Substitute the value of w to get $(3)(2) - 20z = -22$. Then $6 - 20z = -22$, which leads to $-20z = -28$. Finally, $z = \dfrac{28}{20}$, which reduces to $z = \dfrac{7}{5}$ or 1.4.

8 **Example:** *What values of w and z satisfy the system* $\begin{array}{l}2w + 5z = 33\\3w - 2z = -17\end{array}$ *?*

Solution: As in Examples 4–7, adding or subtracting these equations will not "eliminate" either variable. Look at the coefficients of z in the equations. The number 2 does not divide evenly into 5. Is there a number into which both 2 and 5 divide? Yes, there are many such numbers, but let's use the smallest one, namely, 10. If we want $10z$ to appear in the first equation, we must multiply the equation by 2. Similarly, if we want $-10z$ to appear in the second equation, we must multiply the equation by 5. Doing these multiplications, we get the following equations:

$$\begin{array}{r}4w + 10z = 66\\15w - 10z = -85\\\hline 19w = -19\end{array}$$

$$\text{So } w = -1.$$

Notice how the z's dropped out. We now have four different equations into which we can substitute -1 for w.
We will select $2w + 5z = 33$.
We have $(2)(-1) + 5z = 33$.
Then $-2 + 5z = 33$, which leads to $5z = 35$, so $z = 7$.

9 **Example:** *What values of x and y satisfy the system* $\begin{array}{l}-8x + 5y = -8\\6x + 9y = 7\end{array}$ *?*

Solution: A quick inspection shows us that adding or subtracting these equations will not "eliminate" either variable. Let's find a way to "eliminate" the x's. The least common multiple of 8 and 6 is 24. Our plan is to multiply the first equation by 3 and the second equation by 4. The revised system of equations is:

$$\begin{array}{r}-24x + 15y = -24\\24x + 36y = 28\\\hline 51y = 4\end{array}$$

$$\text{So } y = \frac{4}{51}.$$

Substitute this y value into $6x + 9y = 7$. Reduce $(9)\left(\dfrac{4}{51}\right) = \dfrac{36}{51}$ to $\dfrac{12}{17}$. Then $6x + (9)\left(\dfrac{4}{51}\right) = 7$. This becomes $6x + \dfrac{12}{17} = 7$.

Next, multiply $6x + \dfrac{12}{17} = 7$ by 17 to get $102x + 12 = 119$.

Then $102x = 107$, so $x = \dfrac{107}{102}$.

MathFlash!

The approximate decimal answers for example 9 are x ≈ 1.05 and y ≈ 0.08.

Example: **10**   ***What values of w and z satisfy the system $\begin{matrix} w - 2z = 10 \\ 3w - 6z = 30 \end{matrix}$?***

Solution: To eliminate the w's, let's multiply the first equation by –3. The result is $3w - 6z = 30$.

$$
\begin{aligned}
-3w + 6z &= -30 \\
3w - 6z &= \;\;30 \\
\hline
0
\end{aligned}
$$

The result shows 0 = 0!

Whenever this situation occurs, the conclusion is that there are an indefinite number of pairs of answers. For example, if $w = 0$, $z = -5$; if $w = 1$, $z = -4.5$; and so forth. For any value of w, a corresponding value of z exists.

MathFlash!

Another common expression used in place of "indefinite" is "infinite."

Example: *What values of x and y satisfy the system* $\begin{array}{c} 3x + 4y = 5 \\ -6x - 8y = 12 \end{array}$ *?*

11

Solution: We could eliminate the y's by multiplying the first equation by 2. This equation becomes $6x + 8y = 10$.

$$
\begin{array}{r}
6x + 8y = 10 \\
-6x + 8y = 12 \\
\hline
0 = 22
\end{array}
$$

Since this statement can **never** be true, our conclusion is that there is no solution to this system of equations.
You can find pairs of x and y values that satisfy each equation separately, but it is impossible to find a single pair of x and y values that satisfies both equations.

Example: *What values of x and y satisfy the system* $\begin{array}{c} 3x - 4y = 5 \\ x - 8y = 10 \end{array}$ *?*

12

Solution: Let's eliminate the y's by multiplying the first equation by -2. Then the "new" first equation becomes $-6x + 8y = -10$. Add the second equation.

$$
\begin{array}{r}
-6x + 8y = -10 \\
x - 8y = 10 \\
\hline
-5x = 0 \\
x = 0
\end{array}
$$

Substituting 0 for x into the first equation, we get:

$$
\begin{array}{r}
(3)(0) - 4y = 5 \\
0 - 4y = 5 \\
-4y = 5 \\
y = -\dfrac{5}{4} \text{ or } -1.25.
\end{array}
$$

MathFlash!

Be sure you understand that Example 12 does exhibit a single pair of values that represent the solution; namely, x = 0 and y = –1.25. For any system of equations that leads to 0 = 0 (such as Example 10), the conclusion is that there are an indefinite number of pairs of answers. For any system where an impossible situation exists (such as Example 11), the conclusion is that there is no solution.

Test Yourself!

For each of the following systems of equations, determine if there is (a) a single pair of answers, (b) no solution, or (c) an indefinite number of solutions. If there is a single pair of answers, write the actual answers.

1. $x - y = 12$
    $3x + y = 16$ *Answers:* _____

2. $w + y = -6$
    $w + 2y = -8$ *Answers:* _____

3. $6x + y = 9$
    $4x + y = 6$ *Answers:* _____

4. $5x - y = 11$
    $15x - 3y = 30$ *Answers:* _____

5. $3w + 2z = 5$
    $4w + 3z = 1$ *Answers:* _____

Test Yourself! (continued)

6.
$-7w - z = 9$
$4w + 2z = -1$

Answers: _____

7.
$5x + 3y = 39$
$7x - 4y = -11$

Answers: _____

8.
$w - 12z = 8$
$5w - 60z = 40$

Answers: _____

9.
$9w + 2z = 2$
$6w + 9z = 32$

Answers: _____

10.
$-3x + 11y = -2$
$5x + 22y = 7$

Answers: _____

Functions—Part I

In this lesson, we will explore the concepts of a relation and a function, as they apply to sets. Functions are useful in understanding the relationship between two quantities, such as (a) the price per gallon of gasoline with the number of gallons bought, (b) the number of employees in a company with the company's payroll, and (c) the number of minutes of a cell phone conversation with the total cost of the phone call.

Your Goal: When you have completed this lesson, you will be able to recognize the elements that define a relation and a function.

LESSON 23

Functions—Part 1

We begin with the concept of a **relation**. A relation is simply a set (collection) of members that are ordered pairs. Members are also called elements. A set is indicated by braces and is normally assigned a capital letter. Here are some examples of relations:

A = {(5, 7), (9, –1)}. Set A has two elements, namely, (5, 7) and (9, –1).

B = {(p, 4), (peach, z), (0.8, box)}. Set B has three elements, namely, (p, 4), (peach, z), and (0.8, box).

C = {(tree, w), (6, 6), (math, tree), (infinity, sun)}. Set C has four elements.

D = {(shoe, 3), (–2, 5), (shoe, 7), (c, d), (0, 17)}. Set D has five elements.

E = {(a, 10), (b, 10), (c, 11), (d, 12), (e, 13), (f, 10)}. Set E has six elements.

Look at set C. Notice that "tree" appears both as a first part of an element in (tree, w) and as a second part of an element in (math, tree). Also, notice that one of the ordered pairs (elements), namely (6, 6), has the same first and second part.

Now look at set D. Notice that there are two ordered pairs that have the same first element, namely (shoe, 3) and (shoe, 7). Likewise, in set E, there are three ordered pairs that have the same second element, namely, (a, 10), (b, 10), and (f, 10).

In relations, where each element is an ordered pair, some elements may have a shared first part or a shared second part. **We do not repeat any identical elements.** Thus, if a relation consisted of (1, 3) and (1, 3), you would only write this pair once. However, if a relation consisted of (1, 3) and (3, 1), both would be included since they are not identical.

As you study the four relations above, notice that no pair is repeated within the same relation. For example, we could have (2, ace) in set E and (2, ace) in set F, since ordered pairs may occur in more than one set. But you would not have (2, ace) shown twice within the same set.

We now introduce the concepts of domain and range for a relation. The **domain** is the set of all first parts of each ordered pair, and the **range** is the set of all second parts of each ordered pair. Let's explain these definitions as they apply to each of the sets **A**, **B**, **C**, and **D**, that we discussed earlier.

For set **A**, the domain is {5, 9}, and the range is {7, –1}.

For set **B**, the domain is {*p*, peach, 0.8}, and the range is {4, *z*, box}.

For set **C**, the domain is {tree, 6, math, infinity}, and the range is {*w*, 6, tree, sun}.

For set **D**, the domain is {shoe, –2, *c*, 0}, and the range is {3, 5, 7, *d*, 17}.

For set **E**, the domain is {*a*, *b*, *c*, *d*, *e*, *f* }, and the range is {10, 11, 12, 13}.

MathFlash!

For each relation, the domain is itself a set of elements. The same is true for the range. For simplicity in all subsequent examples and exercises in this lesson, the sets with numbers will contain only integers (such as 8, –3, 0). We will not use any decimals or fractions. Incidentally, in naming the domain or range, the order in which the elements are written is not important. For example, we could write the domain of set E as {c, d, a, f, e, b}.

Example: 1

Solution:

Set F: *Given the relation F = {(0, 4), (□0, □5), (–8, 7)}, what is the domain, and what is the range?*

The domain is {0,–8}, and the range is {4, 5, 7}.

Example: 2

Solution:

Set G: *Given the relation G = {(8,–2), (1, 8), (–2, 9), (6, 1), (9, 6)}, what is the domain, and what is the range?*

The domain and the range are both the same, namely, {8, 1, –2, 6, 9}. Remember, the elements can appear in any order.

Example: *Set H:* **Given the relation H = {(apple, 11), (car, 11), (–20, 11),**

3 **(z, 11)}, what is the domain, and what is the range?**

Solution: The domain is {apple, car, –20, z}, and the range is {11}.

MathFlash!

For any relation, the minimum number of elements in the domain or in the range is 1. In fact, the relation may even consist of just one ordered pair.

We are now ready to define a function. A **function** is a special type of relation in which for each element of the domain, there is exactly one assigned element in the range. This means that we inspect the element(s) that comprise the domain. If each of these elements is assigned (i.e., paired with) one element in the range, then the relation is a function. If there is at least one exception, the relation is not a function. Unlike in the game of horseshoes, close doesn't count. <u>A relation either is a function or it is not a function</u>.

Let's look at each of the eight relations that we have discussed in this lesson.

<u>**Set A**</u> has only two elements in its domain, and each of them has been assigned to only one element in its range. This is a function.

<u>**Set B**</u> has three elements in its domain. Each of them has been assigned to only one range element. This is a function.

<u>**Set C**</u> has four elements in its domain. Although the word "tree" appears as an element in both the domain and range, each element in its domain is still only assigned to one element in the range. This is a function.

*The definition of a function does not prohibit a specific element from belonging to each of the domain and range. See **Set C**.*

Set D has four elements in its domain but has five elements in its range. Note that the element "shoe" is paired with each of 3 and 7. This situation violates the rule for a function. This is <u>not</u> a function.

Set E has six elements in its domain, and each of them is assigned to only one element in the range. Even though each of a, b, and f in the domain is assigned to the number 10 in the range, this does not violate the rule governing functions. This is a function.

Set F (Example 1) has two elements in its domain. The number 0 is assigned to each of 4 and 5 in the range. This is <u>not</u> a function.

Set G (Example 2) has five elements in its domain. Each of them is assigned only one element in the range. This is a function. Note that the domain and range may have at least some common elements. In this case, the domain and range are identical.

Set H (Example 3) has four elements in its domain. Each of them is assigned to only one element, which is 11. This qualifies as a function.

Example: *Given the relation {(4, 7), (–9, 0), (□, 1)}, what value(s) could you place in the blank so that it is not a function?*

4

Solution: The only possible values would be 4 or –9. If the number 4 were used, then (4, 7) and (4, 1) would be elements of this relation, in which the number 4 in the domain would be assigned to each of 7 and 1 in the range. Thus, it would not be a function.
Likewise, if –9 were used, then (–9, 0) and (–9, 1) would both be elements of this relation. Since –9 would be assigned to each of 0 and 1, the relation would not be a function.

Example: *Given the relation {(3, 6), (–6, –3), (6, □)}, what values could you place in the blank so that it is a function?*

5

Solution: Anything! Hopefully, you were not hypnotized by this question. Regardless of the value you use in the blank, this relation <u>must</u> be a function.

Test Yourself!

For 1–5, state the domain and the range.

1.   {(0, 4), (12, –1), (–1, 4)}

   Domain: _____   Range: _____

2.   {(*berry, red*), (3, 2), (*green*, –5), (–7, *book*)}

   Domain: _____   Range: _____

3.   {(*a*, 3), (*c*, 1), (*a*, 1), (8, *z*), (*c*, 15)}

   Domain: _____   Range: _____

4.   {(–1, –9), (–9, –1), (2, *king*), (*king*, 4), (10, 10), (30, 30)}

   Domain: _____   Range: _____

5.   {(*z, a*), (*z, b*), (*z, c*), (*z, d*)}

   Domain: _____   Range: _____

6.   Suppose a relation consisted of just one ordered pair. Which one of the following is correct?

   (A) It cannot be a function.

   (B) It must be a function.

   (C) It may be a function, depending on the values chosen.

   (D) Relations cannot have one ordered pair.

7. Suppose a relation consists of two ordered pairs. Which one of the following is correct?

    (A)   It cannot be a function.

    (B)   It must be a function.

    (C)   It may be a function, depending on the values chosen.

    (D)   Relations must have at least three ordered pairs.

8. Given the relation {(*candy, cane*), (*rabbit, foot*), (*peter, pan*), (_____, *foot*)}, and using only the words from the domain of this relation, which one(s) could be used so that this relation is <u>not</u> a function?

    (A)   Only "rabbit"   (C)   "candy" or "peter"

    (B)   Only "candy"   (D)   "cane" or "pan"

9. Given the relation {(*c*, –2), (*d*, 2), (*e*, 3), (*f*, –3) (____, 4)}, in how many different ways can you fill in this blank so that this relation is a function?

    (A)   None   (C)   2

    (B)   1   (D)   An infinite number of ways

10. You are given a function in which the domain has three elements and the range has two elements. Which one of the following satisfies these requirements?

    (A)   {(0, 9), (14, 7), (–5, 8)}

    (B)   {(*berry, red*), (*green, red*), (*green, book*)}

    (C)   {(*d*, 7), (*h*, 1), (*d*, 9), (*h*, 7)}

    (D)   {(–6, *ace*), (–7, *jack*), (–8, *ace*)}

Lesson Twenty-four

Functions—Part 2

In this lesson, we will continue to explore the concept of a function, specifically functional notation and evaluation. We will use *x* and *y* exclusively to represent the variables, although any letters can be used. Applications using formulas will also be shown.

Your Goal: When you have completed this lesson, you will be able to recognize functional notation, understand some of its most useful applications, and calculate numerical answers related to functions.

LESSON 24

Functions—Part 2

You recall that a function is a special type of relation. **Each value of the domain must be paired with only one value in the range.** For this entire lesson, the values of the domain will be represented by the variable x, and the values of the range will be represented by the variable y. Additionally, all domain and range elements will be numbers.

Example: *You are given the formula $y = 5x$. Suppose the allowable values of x are 0, 1, 2, and 3. What are the corresponding values of y? How can these values be written as a function, using ordered pairs?*

1

Solution: Substitute each value of x in order to find the corresponding y value.

If $x = 0$, then $y = (5)(0) = 0$.
If $x = 1$, then $y = (5)(1) = 5$.
If $x = 2$, then $y = (5)(2) = 10$.
If $x = 3$, then $y = (5)(3) = 15$.

This function can be written as {(0, 0), (1, 5), (2, 10), (3, 15)}.

MathFlash!

For Example 1, the domain = {0, 1, 2, 3}, and the range = {0, 5, 10, 15}.

Example:

2

Given the formula $y = -4x + 3$, suppose that the allowable values of x are $-1, \frac{1}{2}, 5,$ and 6.2. What are the corresponding values of y? How can these values be written as a function, using ordered pairs?

Solution: As in Example 1, just substitute the x values into the formula, in order to get the corresponding y values. Here are the computations:

For $x = -1$, $y = (-4)(-1) + 3 = 7$.
For $x = \left(\frac{1}{2}\right)$, $y = (-4)\left(\frac{1}{2}\right) + 3 = -2 + 3 = 1$.
For $x = 5$, $y = (-4)(5) + 3 = -20 + 3 = -17$.
For $x = 6.2$, $y = (-4)(6.2) + 3 = -24.8 + 3 = -21.8$.

This function can be written as $\{(-1, 7), \left(\frac{1}{2}, 1\right), (5, -17), (6.2, -21.8)\}$.

Also, you should be able to identify the set of the given x values as the domain and the set of the computed y values as the range.

Example:

3

Given the formula $y = 3x^2$, suppose that the domain is $\{-4, -1.5, 0, 8\}$. What are the corresponding y values? How can the x and y values be written as a function, using ordered pairs?

Solution: If $x = -4$, then $y = (3)(-4)^2 = (3)(16) = 48$.
If $x = -1.5$, then $y = (3)(-1.5)^2 = (3)(2.25) = 6.75$.
If $x = 0$, then $y = (3)(0)^2 = 0$.
If $x = 8$, then $y = (3)(8)^2 = (3)(64) = 192$.
This function can be written as $\{(-4, 48), (-1.5, 6.75), (0, 0), (8, 192)\}$.

Example: *Given the formula $y = 16 - x^2$, suppose that the domain is $\{-7, -\frac{1}{3}, 1.6, 5\}$. What are the corresponding range values?*

How can the x and y values be written as a function, using ordered pairs?

4

Solution: The range values refer to y values. Just apply substitution for each x value. If $x = -7$, then $y = 16 - (-7)^2 = 16 - 49 = -33$.

If $x = -\frac{1}{3}$, then $y = 16 - \left(-\frac{1}{3}\right)^2 = 16 - \frac{1}{9} = 15\frac{8}{9}$.

If $x = 1.6$, then $y = 16 - (1.6)^2 = 16 - 2.56 = 13.44$.

If $x = 5$, then $y = 16 - (5)^2 = 16 - 25 = -9$.

This function can be written as $\{(-7, -33)\left(-\frac{1}{3}, 15\frac{8}{9}\right)$, $(1.6, 13.44), (5, -9)\}$

At this point, let's introduce **functional notation**. You are given a function involving the variables x and y, where the values of x represent the domain, and the values of y represent the range.

Instead of using the letter y, a common notation is "$f(x)$ to be read as "f of x." This does <u>not</u> mean "f times x." Returning to Example 1, you could have written $f(x) = 5x$. Notice that "$f(x)$" is merely taking the place of y. Here is the advantage of such a notation: Instead of writing "What is the value of y when x is 1?" you can write "What is the value of $f(1)$?" Likewise, instead of writing "If $x = 3$, then $y = $ ____," you can simply write "$f(3) = $ ____."

Also, because there may be more than one function in the problems you will encounter in other math courses, the symbols "$g(x)$" and "$h(x)$" can be used to represent y. Looking at Example 2, instead of writing "$y = -4x + 3$," it would have been just as correct to write "$f(x) = -4x + 3$", "$g(x) = -4x + 3$," or "$h(x) = -4x + 3$."

Thus, if you chose $g(x) = -4x + 3$ for your functional notation, then "$g\left(\frac{1}{2}\right)$" would mean "find the value of the function (that is, the y value) when $x = \frac{1}{2}$. Thus, $g\left(\frac{1}{2}\right) = (-4)\left(\frac{1}{2}\right) + 3 = -2 + 3 = 1$. This is the same value you got when you were seeking the y value, given the x value of $\frac{1}{2}$.

Had you written this function as $h(x) = -4x + 3$, then the value of $h\left(\frac{1}{2}\right)$ would have also been 1.

You just need to recognize that the choice of $f(x)$, $g(x)$, or $h(x)$ is purely arbitrary. In Example 3, you could write $g(x) = 3x^2$. Similarly, in Example 4, you could write $f(x) = 16 - x^2$.

5

Example: Given $f(x) = \dfrac{5}{x}$, find the values of $f(-2)$ and $f\left(\dfrac{1}{3}\right) + f(4)$.

Solution: $f(-2) = \dfrac{5}{-2}$, which can be written as $-\dfrac{5}{2}$.

$f\left(\dfrac{1}{3}\right) + f(4) = \dfrac{5}{\frac{1}{3}} + \dfrac{5}{4} = 15 + \dfrac{5}{4} = \dfrac{65}{4}$.

6

Example: Given $g(x) = x^2 - 10x$, find the values of $g(-0.2)$ and $\dfrac{2}{3} \times g(6)$.

Solution: $g(-0.2) = (-0.2)^2 - (10)(-0.2) = 0.04 + 2 = 2.04$.

$\dfrac{2}{3} \times g(6) = \dfrac{2}{3} \times [(6)^2 - (10)(6)] = \dfrac{2}{3} \times [36 - 60] = \dfrac{2}{3} \times [-24] = -16$.

In all our examples thus far, we were given domain (x) values, and we had to find the corresponding range (y) values. Let's reverse the roles for the next eight examples.

7

Example: Given $f(x) = 3x + 8$, what value of x exists so that $f(x) = 2$?

Solution: Notice that we are actually given the y value of 2. By substitution, $2 = 3x + 8$. For convenience, rewrite the equation as $3x + 8 = 2$, Subtract 8 from each side of the equation to get $3x = -6$, so the answer is $x = -2$.

Let's Review
SEE LESSONS
2 & 3

8

Example: Given $g(x) = \dfrac{3}{4}x - 5$, what value of x exists so that $g(x) = 8$?

Solution: By substitution, $8 = \dfrac{3}{4}x - 5$, which is equivalent to $\dfrac{3}{4}x - 5 = 8$. Add 5 to each side of the equation to get $\dfrac{3}{4}x = 13$. Finally, the answer is $x = 13 \div \dfrac{3}{4} = \dfrac{13}{1} \times \dfrac{4}{3} = \dfrac{52}{3}$.

Example: *Given h(x) = 18x² + 2x, what values of x exist so that h(x) = 0?*

9

Solution: By substitution, $0 = 18x^2 + 2x$, which we will write as $18x^2 + 2x = 0$. Like a good friend whom you once knew, equations such as this one ought to look very familiar!

When we factor the left side of the equation, we get $(2x)(9x + 1) = 0$. If $2x = 0$, then $x = 0$.

If $9x + 1 = 0$, then $x = -\dfrac{1}{9}$. The two answers are 0 or $-\dfrac{1}{9}$.

Let's Review
SEE LESSONS 16-20

MathFlash!

Remember that for equations in which the highest exponent of the variable is 2, you must bring all terms to one side and have zero on the other side. Then, either use factoring or the Quadratic Formula to solve for the answers. Also, for convenience and familiarity, we will switch sides of the equation to ensure that zero is on the right side.

Example: *Given f(x) = x² + 4x –3, what values of x exist so that f(x) = 9?*

10

Solution: Substitute to get $9 = x^2 + 4x - 3$. Subtract 9 from each side. The equation becomes $x^2 + 4x - 12 = 0$. Using Trial and Error Factoring, the equation becomes $(x + 6)(x - 2) = 0$.

If $x + 6 = 0$, then $x = -6$.

If $x - 2 = 0$, then $x = 2$. The two answers are –6 or 2.

11

Example: *Given g(x) = 3x² – 50x + 32, what values of x exist so that g(x) = 0?*

Solution: Substitute to get $3x^2 - 50x + 32 = 0$.
You will need to use some patience and Trial and Error factoring.
Then the equation appears as $(3x - 2)(x - 16) = 0$.
If $3x - 2 = 0$, $3x = 2$, then $x = \dfrac{2}{3}$.
If $x - 16 = 0$, then $x = 16$. The two answers are $\dfrac{2}{3}$ or 16.

12

Example: *Given h(x) = 16x² – 10, what values of x exist so that h(x) = –1?*

Solution: By substitution, we have $-1 = 16x^2 - 10$. Adding 1 to each side, then switching sides, the equation reads as $16x^2 - 9 = 0$.
Using the Difference of Two Squares Factoring, the equation becomes $(4x - 3)(4x + 3) = 0$.
The two answers are $\dfrac{3}{4}$ or $-\dfrac{3}{4}$.

13

Example: *Given f(x) = 5x² + 12x + 19, what values of x exist so that f(x) = 19?*

Solution: Once you substitute, the equation becomes $5x^2 + 12x + 19 = 19$, which simplifies to $5x^2 + 12x = 0$.
Similar to Example 9, Common Term Factoring will be your best method. This leads to $(x)(5x + 12) = 0$. The two answers are 0 or $-\dfrac{12}{5}$.

14

Example: *Given g(x) = x² + 11x + 4, what values of x exist so that g(x) = –3?*

Solution: Substitute –3 to get $-3 = x^2 + 11x + 4$. Adding 3 to each side and switching sides, we get $x^2 + 11x + 7 = 0$. Factoring cannot help us here, so we use the Quadratic Formula.
In this example, $A = 1$, $B = 11$, and $C = 7$.

Let's Review
SEE LESSON 21

By direct substitution, $x = \dfrac{-11 \pm \sqrt{11^2 - (4)(1)(7)}}{(2)(1)}$.
Then since $11^2 - (4)(1)(7) = 121 - 28 = 93$, and $\sqrt{93} \approx 9.64$, the two answers can be approximated by $\dfrac{-11 - 9.64}{2}$ and $\dfrac{-11 + 9.64}{2}$ which reduce to $\dfrac{-21.64}{2}$ and $\dfrac{-1.36}{2}$. The two answers are –10.32 or –0.68.

MathFlash!

Remember that the Quadratic Formula can be used even when factoring is applicable. In Example 11, if you simply could not find the correct factoring for $3x^2 - 50x + 32$, you could always resort to using the Quadratic Formula.

Test Yourself!

1. If $y = -8x + 2$ and the domain is $\{-3, 1, 2, 5\}$, what are the corresponding range values?

   Answers: _____

2. If $y = 2x^2 + 3$ and the domain is $\{-4, -\frac{2}{3}, 1.3, 6\}$, what are the corresponding range values and how is this function written using ordered pairs?

   Range values: _____ *Function:* { _____ }

3. If $f(x) = -\frac{6}{x}$, what is the value of $f(3) + f\left(\frac{1}{3}\right)$?

   Answer: _____

4. If $g(x) = 4x - x^2$, what is the value of $g(-3) + \frac{3}{5} \times g(10)$?

   Answer: _____

5. For which one of the following functions does $f(5) = f(-5)$?

   (A) $f(x) = \frac{x}{5}$ (C) $f(x) = x^2 + x$

   (B) $f(x) = x - 5$ (D) $f(x) = x^2 + 5$

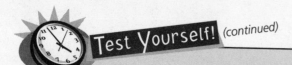 *(continued)*

6.   If $g(x) = -7x + 13$, what value of x exists so that $g(x) = 41$?

      Answer: _____

7.   If $h(x) = \dfrac{5}{8}x + 2$, what value of x exists so that $h(x) = -1$?

      Answer: _____

8.   If $f(x) = x^2 - x - 96$, what values of x exist so that $f(x) = -6$?

      Answers: _____

9.   If $g(x) = 4x^2 - 9x$, what values of x exist so that $g(x) = 0$?

      Answers: _____

10.   If $h(x) = 6x^2 + 5x - 10$, what values of x exist so that $h(x) = 1$?

      Answers: _____

11.   If $f(x) = 16x^2 + 5$, what values of x exist so that $f(x) = 14$?

      Answers: _____

12.   If $g(x) = x^2 - 4x - 6$, what values of x exist so that $g(x) = 0$?
      (You may round off the answers to the nearest hundredth.)

      Answers: _____

LESSONS 21-24

QUIZ FIVE

1. Given the function described by $y = -7x + 2$, if the domain is $\{0, 1, -1\}$, what is the sum of all three range values?

   A −6

   B −2

   C 2

   D 6

2. Which one of the following relations has four elements in its domain and only one element in its range?

   A $\{(a,b), (b,a), (c,d), (d,c)\}$

   B $\{(z,b), (z,a), (z,d), (z,c)\}$

   C $\{(a,z), (b,z), (d,z), (c,z)\}$

   D $\{(z,a), (y,b), (x,c), (w,d)\}$

3. The equation $x^2 - 10x + 3 = 0$ has two answers for x. Which one of the following is one of these answers? (rounded off to the nearest hundredth)

   A −0.31

   B −0.11

   C 0.11

   D 0.31

4. What is the value of y that satisfies the following system of equations?
   $$5x + 3y = 1$$
   $$2x - 3y = -8$$

   A 2

   B 1

   C −1

   D −2

5. Given $g(x) = 4x^2 + 7x + 29$, what values of x exist so that $g(x) = 26$?

   A $-\dfrac{1}{4}$ or −7

   B $-\dfrac{1}{4}$ or −1

   C $-\dfrac{3}{4}$ or −7

   D $-\dfrac{3}{4}$ or −1

6. Given the relation $\{(ace,king), (jack, queen), (\underline{\quad}, jack), (diamond,heart)\}$, which one of the following could be used in the blank space so that this relation is a function?

   A jack

   B queen

   C diamond

   D ace

7. In using the Quadratic Formula to solve for the values of z in the equation $6z^2 + 3z - 2 = 0$, which of these numbers would appear under the square root sign?

   A 57

   B 48

   C 39

   D 26

8. **What is the difference of the values of x that satisfy the equation $x^2 + 3x - 11 = 0$? (rounded off to the nearest hundredth)**

   A   9.14

   B   7.28

   C   5.42

   D   3.56

9. **Which one of the following systems of equations has no solution?**

   A $x + 6y = 10$
         $x + 12y = 20$

   B $x + 4y = 15$
         $3x + 12y = 45$

   C $x + 7y = 11$
         $4x + 28y = 47$

   D $x + 3y = 11$
         $3x + y = 11$

10. **A function is known to consist of two ordered pairs. Which one of the following statements must be true?**

    A   The domain equals the range.

    B   The range consists of two elements.

    C   The domain consists of two elements.

    D   No element appears in both the domain and the range.

CUMULATIVE EXAM

1. Which of the following is one of the factors of $5x^2 - 27x - 18$?

   A $5x - 6$

   B $5x + 3$

   C $x + 6$

   D $x - 3$

2. Ms. Wilson's class is planning to go on a field trip. Each of her students has agreed to cover all expenses. If 32 go, each will pay $18. If 30 of them are actually able to go on the day of the field trip, how much would each of these students have to pay?

   A $21.40

   B $20.00

   C $19.60

   D $19.20

3. In using the Quadratic Formula to solve $3w^2 - 2w - 9 = 0$ for the values of w, what number will appear under the square root sign?

   A 130

   B 112

   C 66

   D 38

4. What is the value of z in the inequality $13 - 3(z + 6) < 16$?

   A $z > 5$

   B $z < 7$

   C $z > -7$

   D $z < -5$

5. Which of the following is equivalent to $(11^6)^8$?

   A 11^{48}

   B 121^{14}

   C 11^{14}

   D 66^8

6. Which of the following expressions is equivalent to $(y^2 + 7)(y - 2)$?

   A $y^3 - 2y^2 + 7y - 14$

   B $y^3 + 2y^2 - 7y - 14$

   C $y^3 + 5y - 14$

   D $y^3 - 5y^2 - 14$

7. A clock company is planning to hire 24 new employees next year. If this represents an employee increase of 15%. What will be the total number of employees next year?

   A 136

   B 160

   C 184

   D 208

8. Given that $x = -5$, what is the value of $8x - 2x^2$?

   A −140

   B −90

   C 10

   D 60

9. The number 63 is 125% larger than what number?

   A 78.75

   B 50.4

   C 28

   D 15.75

10. If -0.68, $-\dfrac{2}{3}$, $-\dfrac{11}{17}$, $-0.\overline{68}$ were arranged in order from smallest to largest, which number would be second?

    A −0.68

    B $-\dfrac{2}{3}$

    C $-\dfrac{11}{17}$

    D $-0.\overline{68}$

11. Given a function in which the domain is {*apple, pear, carrot*} and the range is {*berry, pear, tomato*}, which one of the following could not be an element of this function?

    A (*apple, tomato*)

    B (*pear, pear*)

    C (*carrot, berry*)

    D (*tomato, carrot*)

12. Tammy is buying skirts and pairs of shoes. Each skirt costs $22, and each pair of shoes costs $60. She will spend a maximum of $700. If she decides to buy six skirts, what is the maximum number of pairs of shoes that she can buy?

    A 7

    B 8

    C 9

    D 10

13. The enrollment at a university dropped by 16% from last year to this year. The enrollment this year is 6846 students. What was the enrollment last year?

    A 5751

    B 5900

    C 7941

    D 8150

14. Which one of the following expressions <u>cannot</u> be factored as the difference of two perfect squares?

    A $z^6 - 9$

    B $z^4 - 6$

    C $25 - 64z^2$

    D $49z^4 - 1$

15. The actual distance between Baltimore and Kansas City is 960 miles. The legend of a map of the United States states that $\frac{1}{4}$ inch is equivalent to 30 miles. On this map, how many inches apart are these two cities?

A 24

B 20

C 16

D 8

16. Given $h(x) = \dfrac{12}{x^2}$, what is the value of $h\left(\dfrac{2}{3}\right) + h(-1)$?

A 39

B $17\dfrac{1}{3}$

C 15

D $-6\dfrac{2}{3}$

17. For which one of the following equations is the value of x equal to -15?

A $\dfrac{x}{7} = -\dfrac{7}{15}$

B $-\dfrac{6}{5}x = 18$

C $2x = -\dfrac{15}{2}$

D $-\dfrac{8}{3}x = -40$

18. What is the solution for x in the following system of equations?
$$4x - y = 3$$
$$10x + 3y = 2$$

A $\dfrac{1}{2}$

B 1

C $\dfrac{3}{2}$

D 2

19. Vinny has an unusual dental insurance plan in which he has a $150 deductible. His insurance company will pay 95% of any amount in excess of $150. Recently, he had major dental work for which the bill totaled $3500. How much money will Vinny have to pay?

A $3182.50

B $1925.00

C $317.50

D $175.00

20. For which one of the following expressions would Common Term Factoring involve $6x^2$?

A $27x^2 - 6x^4$

B $18x^3 - 30x^2$

C $42x^3 + 18x$

D $6x^2 + 24$

21. For which one of the following equations, already written in factored form, are the solutions for x equal to $\frac{1}{5}$ or –5?

   A $(5x + 1)(x + 5) = 0$

   B $(5x - 1)(x - 5) = 0$

   C $(5x + 1)(x - 5) = 0$

   D $(5x - 1)(x + 5) = 0$

22. Look at the following graphical representation on the number line.

   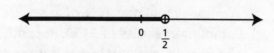

   This represents the solution to which one of the following inequalities?

   A $-6x + 13 > 10$

   B $4x - 11 > -9$

   C $8x + 7 < 3$

   D $-2x - 5 < -4$

23. Given the formula $y = \frac{2}{3}x - 6$, the allowable x values are –12, –6, –3, and 3. Which one of the following is an element of the range?

   A –10

   B –9

   C –6

   D –3

24. What is the factored form of $y^2 - 10y - 24$?

   A $(y - 2)(y + 12)$

   B $(y - 6)(y + 4)$

   C $(y - 12)(y + 2)$

   D $(y - 4)(y + 6)$

25. What is the value of x in the proportion $\frac{\frac{1}{8}}{\frac{3}{4}} = \frac{x}{4}$?

   A $\frac{3}{8}$

   B $\frac{2}{3}$

   C $\frac{3}{2}$

   D $\frac{8}{3}$

Answer Key

1

1. 5.4	$-1.6 + 7$
2. −23	$22 - 45$
3. 22.4	$-1.6 + 24$
4. 2	$21 - 19$
5. 140	$90 + 50$
6. $3\frac{3}{4}$	$-\frac{1}{4} + 5 - 1$
7. −3	$-15 + 12$
8. 102	$81 + 21$
9. −1	$-10 + 1 + 8$
10. 5.24	$3.24 + 2$

2

1. −23	$x = -17 - 6$
2. −80	$y = (20)(-4)$
3. 13	$w = (-65) \div (-5)$
4. $3\frac{2}{3}$	$c = 3 + \frac{2}{3}$
5. $\frac{21}{20}$	$p = \frac{9}{5} - \frac{3}{4} = \frac{36}{20} - \frac{15}{20}$
6. $\frac{3}{10}$	$k = 3 \div 10$
7. −50	$z = (-30)\left(\frac{5}{3}\right)$
8. 7.5	$x = 60 \div 8$
9. $-\frac{3}{35}$	$n = \left(-\frac{3}{7}\right)\left(\frac{1}{5}\right)$
10. $\frac{3}{2}$	$m = \left(\frac{2}{3}\right)\left(\frac{9}{4}\right)$

Lessons

3

1. B   Each part contains xz.
2. D   Subtracting $6t$ from each side leads to $2 = -2$, which is false.
3. -12 $x = (-60) \div 5$
4. 56 $k = (8)(7)$
5. $\dfrac{32}{3}$ $w = \left(2\dfrac{2}{3}\right)(4)$
6. $-\dfrac{25}{4}$ $y = (-25) \div 4$
7. 72 $-\dfrac{1}{6}z = -12$, $z = (-12)(-6)$
8. $\dfrac{3}{8}$ $-8n = -3$, $n = (-3) \div (-8)$
9. $-\dfrac{11}{30}$ $3y = -\dfrac{4}{15} - \dfrac{5}{6} = -\dfrac{33}{30} = -\dfrac{11}{10}$, $y = \left(-\dfrac{11}{10}\right) \div 3$
10. 0.7 $-5c = -3.5$, $c = (-3.5) \div (-5)$

4

1. $x < -2$ $5x < -10$

2. $w < 6$ $-3w > -18$

3. $z > \dfrac{15}{2}$ $4z > 30$

4. $y > -\dfrac{50}{3}$ $-\dfrac{3}{10}y < 5$

5. $x < 4.5$ $0.8x < 3.6$

6. $k \geq -\dfrac{3}{2}$ $\dfrac{3}{4}k \geq -\dfrac{9}{8}$

7. $-6 < c \leq 1$ $30 > -5c \geq -5$

8. $-5 < c < \dfrac{1}{2}$ $20 > -4c > -2$

9. $-\dfrac{13}{12}$ $-1.3 < -1.29 < -\dfrac{6}{5} < -\dfrac{13}{12}$

10. -0.85 $-\dfrac{15}{17} < -\dfrac{6}{7} < -0.85 < -\dfrac{5}{6} < -0.8$

Lessons

5

1. C | For the Associative Property of Multiplication, $(x \times y) \times z = x \times (y \times z)$

2. A | For the Commutative Property of Addition, $x + y = y + x$

3. $x = -\dfrac{3}{2}$ | $30 - 6x = 39, -6x = 9$

4. $x = 6$ | $20 - 9x - 39 = -73, -9x = -54$

5. $y = -\dfrac{11}{4}$ | $16y - 10 = -21 + 12y, 4y = -11$

6. $y = 18$ | $y + 90y - 180 = 0, 10y = 180$

7. $z < -\dfrac{9}{2}$ | $16z + 48 < -24, 16z < -72$

8. $z \geq 2$ | $19 + 20z - 4 \geq 55, 20z \geq 40$

9. $w \geq 28$ | $27 + 3w - 4w - 14 \leq -15, -w \leq -28$

10. $-4 < w < \dfrac{27}{4}$ | $-6 < 48 - 8w < 80, -54 < -8w < 32$

6

1. $(x + 36) + x = 100$ | $2x = 64$ | $x = 32$
2. $40x + (6)(1.60x) = \$644.80$ | $49.6x = \$644.80$ | $x = \$13$
3. $(46)(5) + 7.5x = 710$ | $7.5x = 480$ | $x = 64$ miles per hour
4. $x + 0.20x = \$432$ | $1.20x = \$432$ | $x = \$360$
5. $400 + (0.30)(x - 400) = \$1090$ | $0.30x = \$810$ | $x = \$2700$
6. $0.10x + (0.25)(48) = \$16.20$ | $0.10x = \$4.20$ | $x = 42$
7. $\dfrac{65 + 81 + 46 + 50 + x}{5} = 70$ | $242 + x = 350$ | $x = 108$
8. $(5.00)(x) + (1.50)(4x) = \$572.00$ | $11x = \$572$ | $x = 52$
9. $x - 0.12x = \$33{,}792$ | $0.88x = \$33{,}792$ | $x = \$38{,}400$
10. $x = $ total amount of the bill $(0.95)(x - 1200) = \$342$ $x = \$1560$ | Phyllis paid $\$1200 + (0.05)(\$1560 - \$1200) = \$1200 + (0.05)(\$360) = \$1218$.

Lessons

7

1. $28x > \$120,000 + 12x$ $16x > \$120,000$ $x > 7500$, so at least 7501 games must be sold.

2. $15,000 + 14x \le (1200)(14)$ $14x \le 1800$ $x \le 128\frac{4}{7}$, then round down to 128.

3. $(\$0.08)(120) + (0.11)(x) \le \$17.00$ $0.11x \le \$7.40$ $x \le 67.\overline{27}$, then round down to 67.

4. $15x > \$300 + 9x$ $6x > \$300$ $x > 50$, so Suzanne must make at least 51 visits.

5. $(\$1.40)(21) + (\$2.20)(x) \le \$60$ $\$2.20x \le \$30.60$ $x \le 13.\overline{90}$, then round down to 13.

6. $\$115,000 + 0.14x > \$170,000 + 0.08x$ $0.06x > \$55,000$ $x > \$916,666.\overline{6}$ Thus, she must generate at least $916,667 in sales dollars.

7. $55 + 2.50x > 80 + 1.75x$ $0.75x > 25$ $x > 33.\overline{3}$ Thus, he must travel at least 34 miles.

8. $170 + 106 + 17x \le 1600$ $17x \le 1324$ $x \le 77.88$ Thus, the maximum number of chairs is 77.

8

1. C $\frac{20}{65} = \frac{4}{13}$. The other fractions reduce to $\frac{3}{10}$.

2. $\frac{70}{3}$ $3x = 70$

3. $\frac{75}{2}$ $4x = 150$

4. 0.0045 $16x = 0.072$

5. 2.8 $1.8x = 5.04$

6. $\frac{5}{27}$ $18x = \frac{4}{3} \times \frac{5}{2} = \frac{10}{3}$

7. 3 $\frac{4}{3}x = \frac{36}{1} \times \frac{1}{9} = 4$

8. $\frac{24}{5}$ $\frac{1}{8}x = \frac{2}{3} \times \frac{9}{10} = \frac{3}{5}$

9. 24 $5x - 75 = 3x - 27$, $2x = 48$

10. $\frac{26}{3}$ $10x = 4x + 52$, $6x = 52$

9

1. $\dfrac{96}{x} = \dfrac{28}{100}$ $28x = 9600$ 342.86

2. $\dfrac{0.24}{0.5} = \dfrac{x}{100}$ $0.5x = 24$ 48%

3. $\dfrac{200.55}{x} = \dfrac{105}{100}$ $105x = 20{,}055$ 191

4. $\dfrac{x}{84} = \dfrac{1.3}{100}$ $100x = 109.2$ 1.092

5. $\dfrac{x}{60} = \dfrac{88.5}{100}$ $100x = 5310$ 53.1

6. $\dfrac{44}{x} = \dfrac{280}{100}$ $280x = 4400$ 15.71

7. $\dfrac{4.5}{21} = \dfrac{x}{100}$ $21x = 450$ 21.43%

8. $\dfrac{19.6}{9.8} = \dfrac{x}{100}$ $9.8x = 1960$ 200%

9. $\dfrac{x}{120} = \dfrac{100.45}{100}$ $100x = 12{,}054$ 120.54

10. $\dfrac{364}{x} = \dfrac{40}{100}$ $40x = 36{,}400$ 910

Lessons

10

1. $\dfrac{422}{x} = \dfrac{105.5}{100}$ $105.5x = 42{,}200$ 400

2. $\dfrac{x}{360} = \dfrac{78}{100}$ $100x = 28{,}080$ \$280.80

3. $\dfrac{98}{600} = \dfrac{x}{100}$ $600x = 9800$ 16.3%

4. $\dfrac{x}{1100} = \dfrac{116.25}{100}$ $100x = 127{,}875$ \$1278.75

5. $\dfrac{5.4}{18.6} = \dfrac{x}{100}$ $18.6x = 540$ 29%

6. $\dfrac{352}{x} = \dfrac{11}{100}$ $11x = 35{,}200$ \$3200

7. $\dfrac{77}{35} = \dfrac{x}{100}$ $35x = 7700$ 220%

8. $\dfrac{x}{12{,}000} = \dfrac{75.3}{100}$ $100x = 903{,}600$ 9036

9. $\dfrac{48}{128} = \dfrac{x}{100}$ $128x = 4800$ 37.5%

10. $\dfrac{324}{x} = \dfrac{18}{100}$ $18x = 32{,}400$ \$1800

Lessons

11

1. $\dfrac{70}{x} = \dfrac{8}{7}$ $8x = 490$ 61.25

2. $\dfrac{32}{x} = \dfrac{5}{123}$ $5x = 3936$ 787

3. $\dfrac{20}{225} = \dfrac{8}{x}$ $20x = 1800$ 90

4. $\dfrac{430}{510} = \dfrac{19{,}350}{x}$ $430x = 9{,}868{,}500$ \$22,950

5. $\dfrac{400}{330} = \dfrac{65}{x}$ $400x = 21{,}450$
and round <u>down</u>   53

6. $\dfrac{25}{x} = \dfrac{680}{1025}$ $680x = 25{,}625$ 37.68

7. $\dfrac{16}{36} = \dfrac{44}{x}$ $16x = 1584$ 99

8. $\dfrac{344{,}000}{x} = \dfrac{5160}{9288}$ $5160x = 3{,}195{,}072{,}000$ \$619,200

9. $\dfrac{10}{x} = \dfrac{13}{100}$ $13x = 1000$ 77

10. $\dfrac{\frac{1}{6}}{\frac{3}{8}} = \dfrac{1\frac{1}{2}}{x}$ $\dfrac{1}{6}x = \dfrac{9}{16}$ $3\dfrac{3}{8}$

Lessons

12

1. B | Use the reverse operation. | It gets divided by 4.
2. $\dfrac{2.75}{2.95} = \dfrac{x}{8}$ | $2.95x = 22$ | 7.46
3. $\dfrac{20}{x} = \dfrac{8.96}{5.6}$ | $8.96x = 112$ | 12.5
4. $\dfrac{75}{x} = \dfrac{230}{280}$ | $230x = 21{,}000$ | 91.3
5. $\dfrac{30}{25} = \dfrac{x}{\$12.50}$ | $25x = \$375$, $x = \$15$
 Then, $\$15 - \$12.50$ | $ 2.50
6. $\dfrac{12}{x} = \dfrac{8}{18}$ | $8x = 216$ | 27
7. $\dfrac{21.5}{25} = \dfrac{x}{10}$ | $25x = 215$ | 8.6 cubic inches
8. $\dfrac{1960}{1850} = \dfrac{x}{3.40}$ | $1850x = 6664$ | $3.60
9. $\dfrac{120}{x} = \dfrac{60}{45}$ | $60x = 5400$ | 90 amperes
10. $\dfrac{6400}{8000} = \dfrac{x}{36}$ | $8000x = 230{,}400$ | $28.80

13

1. B | Keep the base of 7 and add exponents.
2. C | Keep the base of 9 and subtract exponents.
3. A | Keep the base of 36 and multiply exponents.
4. x^{15} | Add exponents.
5. y^{20} | Subtract exponents.
6. w^{35} | Multiply exponents.
7. z^{17} | $z = z^{1}$. Add exponents.
8. x^{24} | Subtract exponents.
9. y^{23} | Add exponents.
10. z^{40} | Multiply exponents.

Lessons

14

1. $-16x - 4$ $(-4)(4x) + (-4)(1)$

2. $24y^2 - 16y$ $(8y)(3y) - (8y)(2)$

3. $-10z^3 - 3z^2$ $(-z^2)(10z) + (-z^2)(3)$

4. $5w^2 + 55w - 30$ $(5)(w^2) + (5)(11w) + (5)(-6)$

5. $-3y^4 - 36y^2 + 15y$ $(-3y)(y^3) + (-3y)(12y) + (-3y)(-5)$

6. $z^2 - z - 72$ $(z)(z) + (-9)(z) + (8)(z) + (8)(-9)$

7. $4x^2 - 12x - 91$ $(2x)(2x) + (7)(2x) + (-13)(2x) + (-13)(7)$

8. $6w^2 - 11w + 4$ $(-3w)(-2w) + (-3w)(1) + (4)(-2w) + (4)(1)$

9. $4y^3 - 24y^2 - y + 6$ $(4y^2)(y) + (4y^2)(-6) + (-1)(y) + (-1)(-6)$

10. $5x^4 + 62x^2 + 24$ $(x^2)(5x^2) + (x^2)(2) + (12)(5x^2) + (12)(2)$

15

1. $5x^3 - 2x$ $\dfrac{15x^3}{3} - \dfrac{6x}{3}$

2. $4x^2 + 9x$ $\dfrac{20x^2}{5} + \dfrac{45x}{5}$

3. $3x^2 + 2$ $\dfrac{30x^3}{10x} + \dfrac{20x}{10x}$

4. $8y^3 - 1$ $\dfrac{16y^4}{2y} - \dfrac{2y}{2y}$

5. $4y^2 - \dfrac{1}{2}$ $\dfrac{56y^4}{14y^2} - \dfrac{7y^2}{14y^2}$

6. $w^2 - \dfrac{4}{3}w - 11$ $\dfrac{6w^2}{6} - \dfrac{8w}{6} - \dfrac{66}{6}$

7. $\dfrac{1}{3}w^3 + \dfrac{2}{3}w^2 - 3$ $\dfrac{3w^4}{9w} + \dfrac{6w^3}{9w} - \dfrac{27w}{9w}$

8. $5z^2 + 9z - \dfrac{7}{10}$ $\dfrac{50z^4}{10z^2} + \dfrac{90z^3}{10z^2} - \dfrac{7z^2}{10z^2}$

9. $12z^2 - 8z + 14$ $\dfrac{36z^3}{3z} - \dfrac{24z^2}{3z} + \dfrac{42z}{3z}$

10. B   The denominator has two terms.

Lessons

16

1. $(3y)(y + 4)$ — Common term factor of $3y$
2. $(5x^2)(2 - 5x)$ — Common term factor of $5x^2$
3. $(6y)(1 + 7y^2)$ — Common term factor of $6y$
4. $(w)(w^2 - 4w + 11)$ — Common term factor of w
5. $(4)(5z^2 + 2)$ — Common term factor of 4
6. $(9)(y - 6)$ — Common term factor of 9
7. $(3)(2x^2 - 6x - 11)$ — Common term factor of 3
8. $(8z^2)(2z^2 - 7)$ — Common term factor of $8z^2$
9. $(7w)(1 + w + 5w^2)$ — Common term factor of $7w$
10. $(2z)(6z^3 - 5 + 13z)$ — Common term factor of $2z$

17

1. $(x - 6)(x + 6)$ — Difference of two perfect squares
2. $(7z - 10)(7z + 10)$ — Difference of two perfect squares
3. $(5 - 2w^2)(5 + 2w^2)$ — Write as $25 - 4w^4$. Then, difference of two perfect squares
4. $(7)(w - 9)(w + 9)$ — Write as $(7)(w^2 - 81)$. Then, difference of two perfect squares
5. $(z)(z - 3)(z + 3)$ — Write as $(z)(z^2 - 9)$. Then, difference of two perfect squares
6. $(x^2 - 2)(x^2 + 2)$ — Difference of two perfect squares
7. $(y^3 - 4)(y^3 + 4)$ — Difference of two perfect squares
8. $(4x^2)(1 - 3x)(1 + 3x)$ — Write as $(4x^2)(1 - 9x^2)$. Then, difference of two perfect squares
9. $(7 - z)(7 + z)$ — Write as $49 - z^2$. Then, difference of two perfect squares
10. $(60y^3)(y - 1)(y + 1)$ — Write as $(60y^3)(y^2 - 1)$. Then, difference of two perfect squares

Lessons

18

1. $(x + 4)(x + 5)$ $4+ 5 = 9$ and $(4)(5) = 20$

2. $(y - 3)(y + 6)$ $(-3) + (6) = 3$ and $(-3)(6) = -18$

3. $(w - 5)(w - 9)$ $(-5) + (-9) = -14$ and $(-5)(-9) = 45$

4. $(z - 10)(z + 3)$ $(-10) + 3 = -7$ and $(-10)(3) = -30$

5. $(x - 7)(x + 8)$ $(-7) + (8) = 1$ and $(-7)(8) = -56$

6. $(w - 1)(w - 32)$ $(-1) + (-32) = -33$ and $(-1)(-32) = 32$

7. $(z - 2)(z - 7)$ $(-2) + (-7) = -9$ and $(-2)(-7) = 14$

8. $(y - 12) (y + 4)$ $(-12) + (4) = -8$ and $(-12)(4) = -48$

9. $(x - 9)(x - 11)$ $(-9) + (-11) = -20$ and $(-9)(-11) = 99$

10. $(w - 3)(w + 13)$ $(-3) + (13) = 10$ and $(-3)(13) = -39$

19

1. $(5x + 13)(x + 1)$ $(5x)(x) = 5x^2$, $(5x)(1) + (13)(x) = 18x$, and $(13)(1) = 13$

2. $(7)(w - 2)(w - 2)$ Write as $(7)(w^2 - 4w + 4)$. Then, do perfect trinomial square factoring.

3. $(3z - 5)(2z + 1)$ $(3z)(2z) = 6z^2$, $(3z)(1) + (-5)(2z) = -7z$, and $(-5)(1) = -5$

4. $(2y - 3)(2y - 7)$ $(2y)(2y) = 4y^2$, $(2y)(-7) + (-3)(2y) = -20y$, and $(-3)(-7) = 21$

5. $(11)(w - 1)(w + 8)$ Write as $(11)(w^2 + 7w - 8)$. Then, $(w)(w) = w^2$, $(w)(8) + (-1)(w) = 7w$, and $(-1)(8) = -8$

6. $(2z - 5)(z - 4)$ $(2z)(z) = 2z^2$, $(2z)(-4) + (-5)(z) = -13z$, and $(-5)(-4) = 20$

7. $(3)(4x - 3)(2x + 1)$ Write as $(3)(8x^2 - 2x - 3)$, Then, $(4x)(2x) = 8x^2$, $(4x)(1) + (-3)(2x) = -2x$, and $(-3)(1) = -3$

8. $(10w + 1)(w + 6)$ $(10w)(w) = 10w^2$, $(10w)(6) + (1)(w) = 61w$, and $(1)(6) = 6$

9. $(3x - 7)(x + 9)$ $(3x)(x) = 3x^2$, $(3x)(9) + (-7)(x) = 20x$, and $(-7)(9) = -63$

10. $(5)(3z - 2)(3z - 2)$ Write as $(5)(9z^2 - 12z + 4)$. Then, do perfect trinomial square factoring.

Lessons

20

1. $(y - 6)(y + 5) = 0$ $y - 6 = 0$ or $y + 5 = 0$ $6, -5$

2. $(3)(2x - 5)(2x + 5) = 0$ $2x - 5 = 0$ or $2x + 5 = 0$ $\dfrac{5}{2}, -\dfrac{5}{2}$

3. $(w)(w - 14) = 0$ $w = 0$ or $w - 14 = 0$ $0, 14$

4. $(6x - 5)(x - 3) = 0$ $6x - 5 = 0$ or $x - 3 = 0$ $\dfrac{5}{6}, 3$

5. $(2)(z + 11)(z - 2) = 0$ $z + 11 = 0$ or $z - 2 = 0$ $-11, 2$
   $2 \neq 0$

6. $(3)(3y + 2)(y + 8) = 0$ $3y + 2 = 0$ or $y + 8 = 0$ $-\dfrac{2}{3}, -8$
   $3 \neq 0$

7. $(7x - 9)(x - 1) = 0$ $7x - 9 = 0$ or $x - 1 = 0$ $\dfrac{9}{7}, 1$

8. $(4)(w + 7)(w + 7) = 0$ $w + 7 = 0, 4 \neq 0$ -7

9. $(3y)(5y - 3) = 0$ $3y = 0$ or $5y - 3 = 0$ $0, \dfrac{3}{5}$

10. $(z - 9)(5z + 3) = 0$ $z - 9 = 0$ or $5z + 3 = 0$ $9, -\dfrac{3}{5}$

Lessons

1. $\dfrac{12 \pm \sqrt{144 - (4)(1)(-5)}}{2}$ −0.41, 12.41

2. $\dfrac{-18 \pm \sqrt{324 - (4)(1)(-11)}}{2}$ −18.59, 0.59

3. $\dfrac{-9 \pm \sqrt{81 - (4)(1)(10)}}{2}$ −7.70, −1.30

4. Rewrite the equation as $z^2 - 7z + 4 = 0$

$\dfrac{7 \pm \sqrt{49 - (4)(1)(4)}}{2}$ 0.63, 6.37

5. $\dfrac{-5 \pm \sqrt{25 - (4)(4)(-17)}}{8}$ −2.78, 1.53

6. $\dfrac{13 \pm \sqrt{169 - (4)(2)(9)}}{4}$ 0.79, 5.71

7. Rewrite the equation as $3y^2 - y - 9 = 0$

$\dfrac{1 \pm \sqrt{1 - (4)(3)(-9)}}{6}$ −1.57, 1.91

8. Rewrite the equation as $5z^2 + 2z - 4 = 0$

$\dfrac{-2 \pm \sqrt{4 - (4)(5)(-4)}}{10}$ −1.12, 0.72

9. Rewrite the equation as $3x^2 - 19x + 10 = 0$

$\dfrac{19 \pm \sqrt{361 - (4)(3)(10)}}{6}$ 0.58, 5.75

10. Rewrite the equation as $4w^2 + 2w - 3 = 0$

$\dfrac{-2 \pm \sqrt{4 - (4)(4)(-3)}}{8}$ −1.15, 0.65

Lessons

22

1. Add equations to get $4x = 28$. Substitute the x value into first equation to get $7 - y = 12$.

   $x = 7, y = -5$

2. Subtract equations to get $-y = 2$. Substitute the y value into first equation to get $w - 2 = -6$.

   $w = -4, y = -2$

3. Subtract equations to get $2x = 3$. Substitute the x value into first equation to get $(6)(1.5) + y = 9$.

   $x = 1.5, y = 0$

4. Multiply the first equation by 3 to get $15x - 3y = 33$. Subtract the second equation to get $0 = 3$.

   No solution

5. Multiply the first equation by 3 and the second equation by 2 to get $9w + 6z = 15$ and $8w + 6z = 2$, respectively. Subtract to get $w = 13$. Substitute the w value into the first equation to get $(3)(13) + 2z = 5$.

   $w = 13, z = -17$

6. Multiply the first equation by 2 to get $-14w - 2z = 18$. Add to the second equation to get $-10w = 17$. Substitute the w value into the first equation to get $(-7)(-1.7) - z = 9$.

   $w = -1.7, z = 2.9$

7. Multiply the first equation by 4 and the second equation by 3 to get $20x + 12y = 156$ and $21x - 12y = -33$, respectively. Add to get $41x = 123$. Substitute the x value into the first equation to get $(5)(3) + 3y = 39$.

   $x = 3, y = 8$

8. Multiply the first equation by 5 to get $5w - 60z = 40$. Subtract to get $0 = 0$.

   Indefinite number of solutions

9. Multiply the first equation by 9 and the second equation by 2 to get $81w + 18z = 18$ and $12w + 18z = 64$, respectively. Subtract to get $69w = -46$. Substitute the w value into the first equation to get $(9)\left(-\dfrac{2}{3}\right) + 2z = 2$.

   $w = -\dfrac{2}{3}, z = 4$

10. Multiply the first equation by 2 to get $-6x + 22y = -4$. Subtract to get $-11x = -11$. Substitute the x value into the first equation to get $(-3)(1) + 11y = -2$.

   $x = 1, y = \dfrac{1}{11}$

Lessons

23

1. Domain = {0, 12, –1}, Range = {4, –1}

2. Domain = {berry, 3, green, –7}, Range = {red, 2, –5, book}

3. Domain = {*a*, *c*, 8}, Range = {3, 1, *z*, 15}

4. Domain = {–1, –9, 2, king, 10, 30}, Range = {–9, –1, king, 4, 10, 30}

5. Domain = {*z*}, Range = {*a*, *b*, *c*, *d*}

6. B   If there is only one ordered pair, (*x*, *y*), then the value of *x* is assigned to only one value of *y*.

7. C   For example, {(2,3), (1,5)} is a function. However, {(2,3), (2,6)} is not a function.

8. C   If either "candy" or "peter" were substituted into the blank, there would exist two ordered pairs such that a given element of the domain would correspond to two different elements of the range. For example, (candy, cane) and (candy, foot) would both be part of this relation.

9. D   The only exclusions to filling in the blank would be *c*, *d*, *e*, or *f*.

10. D   The domain consists of –6, –7, and –8; the range consists of ace and jack.

Lessons

24

1. The range values are found by evaluating
$(-8)(-3) + 2$, $(-8)(1) + 2$, $(-8)(2) + 2$, and $(-8)(5) + 2$

26, −6, −14, −38

2. $\{(-4,35), \left(-\dfrac{2}{3}, 3\dfrac{8}{9}\right), (1.3, 6.38), (6,75)\}$

$35, 3\dfrac{8}{9}, 6.38, 75$

3. $-\dfrac{6}{3} + \dfrac{-6}{\dfrac{1}{3}} = -2 - 18$

−20

4. $g(-3) = (4)(-3) - (-3)^2 = -21$ and
$g(10) = (4)(10) - (10)^2 = -60$.

Then, find the value of $-21 + \left(\dfrac{3}{5}\right)(-60) = -21 - 36$

−57

5. $(5)^2 + 5 = (-5)^2 + 5 = 30$

D

6. $41 = -7x + 13$, $28 = -7x$

−4

7. $-1 = \dfrac{5}{8}x + 2$, $-3 = \dfrac{5}{8}x$

$-4\dfrac{4}{5}$

8. $-6 = x^2 - x - 96$, $0 = x^2 - x - 90$, $0 = (x + 9)(x - 10)$

−9 or 10

9. $0 = 4x^2 - 9x$, $0 = (x)(4x - 9)$

0 or $\dfrac{9}{4}$

10. $1 = 6x^2 + 5x - 10$, $0 = 6x^2 + 5x - 11$, $0 = (6x + 11)(x - 1)$

$-\dfrac{11}{6}$ or 1

11. $14 = 16x^2 + 5$, $0 = 16x^2 - 9$, $0 = (4x + 3)(4x - 3)$

$-\dfrac{3}{4}$ or $\dfrac{3}{4}$

12. $0 = x^2 - 4x - 6$, $x = \dfrac{4 \pm \sqrt{16 + 24}}{2}$, $x \approx \dfrac{4 \pm 6.32}{2}$

−1.16 or 5.16

Quizzes

1

1. C $-\dfrac{13}{3} < -4\dfrac{1}{4} < -4.12 < -4.\overline{1}$

2. A $(10)\left(\dfrac{2}{5}\right) - \dfrac{20}{\frac{2}{5}} + 1 = 4 - 50 + 1$

3. D $x \times y = y \times x$. In this example, $x = 7$ and $y = 2$

4. A $(4)(-5) - 3(-5)^2 = -20 - 75$

5. B $k = 30 - \dfrac{5}{6}$

6. C $5 + 24 - 4z > 28,\ -4z > -1$

7. B yw^2 and w^2y are like terms. Same letters with the same corresponding exponents

8. A $-40 < 5c < -20$

9. D $9n = \dfrac{5}{8},\ n = \dfrac{5}{8} \times \dfrac{1}{9}$

10. B $x + \dfrac{1}{9} = \dfrac{1}{9}$ simplifies to $x = \dfrac{1}{9} - \dfrac{1}{9}$

2

1. B $\left(\dfrac{1.5}{13.5}\right)(100)\%$

2. C $0.8x = 2.88$

3. A $30x + (6)(1.6x) = \$475.20,\ 39.6x = \$475.20$

4. D $15x - 45 = 11x,\ -45 = -4x$

5. C $0.15x = 87,\ x = \$580,\ \$580 + \$87$

6. B $(\$24)(7) + \$12x \le \$450,\ x \le 23.5$

7. B $100\% - 32.5\% = 67.5\% = 0.675$. Then $(50)(0.675)$

8. C $100\% - 18\% = 82\% = 0.82$ Then $(\$420)(0.82)$

9. D $\$45x \ge \$150{,}000 + \$24x,\ x \ge \dfrac{150{,}000}{21}$

10. A $1400 - 1380 = 20$. Then $\left(\dfrac{2}{1380}\right)(100)\%$

Quizzes

3

1. D $(2y^2)(y^2) + 5y^2 - 16y^2 - 40$

2. B $\dfrac{\$2.60}{x} = \dfrac{19}{16}.$ $19x = \$41.6$

3. C $\dfrac{\$56}{x} = \dfrac{300}{675}.$ $300x = \$37,800$

4. B $\dfrac{\frac{3}{8}}{x} = \dfrac{1\frac{1}{2}}{2\frac{1}{4}}.$ $1\frac{1}{2}x = \dfrac{27}{32}$

5. A   The exponent for w will be $(4)(3) - 4$

6. C $\dfrac{55}{62} = \dfrac{x}{262}.$ $62x = 14,410$

7. A $\dfrac{24x}{24x} + \dfrac{72x^4}{24x}$

8. D $(3z)(-5z) + 6z + 20z - 8$

9. B $\dfrac{16w^2}{4w^2} - \dfrac{12w^4}{4w^2} + \dfrac{32w^6}{4w^2}$

10. C   Keep the base of 64 and the exponent is $30 - 3$

4

1. A $(3)(w^2 + 2w - 63) = (3)(w + 9)(w - 7)$, $w + 9 = 0$, $w - 7 = 0$.

2. B   Trinomial factoring. Two numbers whose product is -84 and whose sum is -8 are -14 and $+6$.

3. D   Common term factoring with $2z$ as the common factor.
$\dfrac{2z^3}{2z} = z^2, \dfrac{-18z^2}{2z} = -9z, \dfrac{6z}{2z} = 3$

4. B $(20x)(x) = 20x^2$, $(20x)(-4) - 7x = -87x$, $(-1)(-28) = 28$

5. C $(6)(w^2 + 9w + 20) = (6)(w + 5)(w + 4)$

6. C $(x)(25x^2 - 16)$, then use difference of two squares factoring.

7. D $(3y)(6y - 1) = 0$, $3y = 0$, $6y - 1 = 0$.

8. A   Common term factoring, using 4 as a common term.
$(4)(w^2 - w - 1)$.

9. C $100y^2 - 9 = (10y - 3)(10y + 3)$

10. A   The greatest common factor of 30 and 18 is 6, and the greatest common factor of x^3 and x^4 is x^3.

Quizzes

5

1. D   The range values are 2, –5, and 9.

2. C   The domain consists of a, b, c, d. The range consists of z

3. D   The two answers are $\dfrac{10 \pm \sqrt{88}}{2} \approx 0.31$ and 9.69

4. A   Add equations to get $7x = -7$, so $x = -1$.
   Substitute into the first equation to get $-5 + 3y = 1$.

5. D $4x^2 + 7x + 3 = 0$, $(4x + 3)(x + 1) = 0$

6. B   Using "queen" in the blank space would result in four different domain values.

7. A $z = \dfrac{-3 \pm \sqrt{3^2 - (4)(6)(-2)}}{12}$. Then $3^2 - (4)(6)(-2) = 57$.

8. B   The two answers are $z = \dfrac{-3 \pm \sqrt{53}}{2} \approx 2.14$ and -5.14

9. C   Multiply the first equation by 4 to get $4x + 28y = 44$.
   Subtract the second equation to get $0 = -3$.

10. C   In order to qualify as a function, the elements of the domain must be different.

Cumulative Exam

1. B   The factors are $5x + 3$ and $x - 6$. (Factoring)

2. D   ($32)(18) \div 30$ (Inverse Variation)

3. B $w = \dfrac{2 \pm \sqrt{(-2)^2 - (4)(3)(-9)}}{6}$. $(-2)^2 - (4)(3)(-9) = 112$

             (Quadratic Formula)

4. C $13 - 3z - 18 < 16$, $-3z < 21$ (Solving Inequalities)

5. A   Keep the same base and multiply the exponents. (Rules of Exponents)

6. A $(y^2)(y) + (-2)(y^2) + (7)(y) + (7)(-2)$ (Multiplying Expressions)

7. C $24 \div 0.15 = 160$, then $160 + 24$ (Percent Increase)

8. B $(8)(-5) - 2(-5)^2 = -40 - 50$ (Evaluating Expressions)

9. C $63 \div 2.25$ (Percent Increase)

10. A $-0.\overline{68} < -0.68 < -\dfrac{2}{3} < -\dfrac{11}{17}$ (Ordering of Numbers)

11. D   Each element is an ordered pair, in which the first part is an element of the domain and the second part is an element of the range. (Domain, Range)

12. C $(6)($22) + $60x \le 700. Round <u>down</u> to the nearest integer. (Solving Inequalities)

13. D $6846 \div 0.84$ (Percent Decrease)

14. B $z^4 = (z^2)(z^2)$, but 6 is not a perfect square. (Factoring)

15. D $\dfrac{960}{30} = \dfrac{x}{\frac{1}{4}}$. (Direct Variation)

16. A $\dfrac{12}{\left(\frac{2}{3}\right)^2} + \dfrac{12}{(-1)^2} = 27 + 12 = 39$ (Evaluating Functions)

17. B $x = (18)\left(-\dfrac{5}{6}\right) = -15$ (Solving Proportions)

18. A   Multiply the first equation by 3 to get $12x - 3y = 9$. Add the second equation to get $22x = 11$. (Simultaneous Equations in Two Variables)

19. C $$150 + (0.05)(3350)$ (Word Problems on Percents)

Cumulative Exam

20. B $6x^2$ divides evenly into each of $18x^3$ and $30x^2$ (Factoring)

21. D   If $5x - 1 = 0$, $x = \dfrac{1}{5}$ and if $x + 5 = 0$, $x = -5$

(Solving Equations by Factoring)

22. A $-6x > -3$ becomes $x < \dfrac{1}{2}$. Graphically, put a circle around $\dfrac{1}{2}$ and draw an arrow to the left. (Solving Inequalities)

23. A   The range values are -14, -10, -8, -4. (Domain, Range)

24. C   The two numbers that add up to -10 and whose product is -24 are -12 and $+2$. (Factoring)

25. B $\dfrac{3}{4}x = \dfrac{1}{2}$. Then $x = \left(\dfrac{1}{2}\right)\left(\dfrac{4}{3}\right)$. (Solving Proportions)

Workspace

Workspace

Workspace

Workspace

Workspace

Workspace

SCORECARD

Algebra & Functions

Lesson	Completed	Number of Drill Questions	Number Correct	What I need to review...
1		10		
2		10		
3		10		
4		10		
5		10		
6		10		
7		8		
8		10		
9		10		
10		10		
11		10		
12		10		
13		10		
14		10		
15		10		
16		10		
17		10		
18		10		
19		10		
20		10		
21		10		
22		10		
23		10		
24		12		

Quiz		What I need to review...
1	/10	
2	/10	
3	/10	
4	/10	
5	/10	

Cumulative Exam	/25	